**THE BOSS** who interrupts or ignores a staff member's comments during meetings . . .

**THE COWORKER** who passes on juicy gossip—purely for political reasons . . .

**THE MANAGER** who always seems to be hiding behind closed doors . . .

They all have something in common: a lack of people skills. Without the ability to handle interpersonal situations wisely, we sabotage our own success—and when others are causing the problems, we need to know how to solve them *without* resorting to rudeness, resentment, and political maneuvering. This is the book that shows you how!

# SAY THE MAGIC WORDS

# SAY THE MAGIC WORDS

## RICHARD E. BYRD, Ph.D.

BERKLEY BOOKS, NEW YORK

*To Bill, Bob, and Dan,*
*who were gracious even*
*in the '70s*

SAY THE MAGIC WORDS

A Berkley Book / published by arrangement with
the author

PRINTING HISTORY
Berkley edition / November 1993

ISBN: 0-425-13986-7

BERKLEY®
Berkley Books are published by The Berkley Publishing Group,
200 Madison Avenue, New York, New York 10016.
BERKLEY and the "B" design
are trademarks belonging to Berkley Publishing Corporation.

PRINTED IN THE UNITED STATES OF AMERICA

10  9  8  7  6  5  4  3  2  1

# CONTENTS

*

# *
# Acknowledgments

FIRST OF ALL, I'd like to acknowledge and thank my many clients of the past twenty-five-plus years for providing much of the wheat and some of the chaff that make up this book. Mixed with some basic Judeo-Christian principles I was given as a boy, the result is bread for those who truly believe that people are any company's most important asset.

This bread would still be in the oven, however, except for the kneading and patting into shape by Andrew Zack, my original editor at Berkley. He read it so many times that he actually began to think the book was too short.

Way back when, long before our Berkley editors, there were many others. There was Sheldon Busansky who provided the first opportunity for me to present the original ideas to his management team. And Phyllis Busansky was the first to tell me the ideas actually changed some of her management practices.

That was real encouragement. Scott Edelstein, another longtime friend and editor, applied his talents to a very early version of this book. My thanks to each of them.

I also need to thank all those who gave me stories out of their experiences, some of whom read the early draft and said "Right on!" This list includes Susan Eilertsen, Sandra Hale, Gary Fink, Janet Fiola, Marv Segal, Kate O'Keefe, Tim Signorelli, Bill Gjetson, and Dave Larson.

In the final months of preparing this material for the publisher, another longtime friend and editor, David Martin, worked with me on the newer material to sift out overlaps, repair sentences that didn't make sense, reduce inconsistencies, and otherwise cover up my missteps. He's always believed in the book, and for that I'm thankful.

I'm grateful to Doris Schnable who spent many an hour struggling to decipher my handwritten hieroglyphics as she typed, retyped, and re-retyped this manuscript. She was always a good sport and ready for the challenge of a new chapter.

Marj Hutchinson, my good friend and the business manager of my consulting firm, who takes much of my other wheat and chaff writings and makes bread of them, also worked over the manuscript many times. What would I do without her sometimes devastating honesty? For example, "Why write this book? Isn't it stating the obvious?" To her, some of the real-life stories were so bizarre that there was no point in including them. "Readers will think you made them up," she said. But she kept us to the recipe as she second-guessed all of us on detail and form as well as issues of substance.

One clear sponsor of this book, who believed it was needed, is my wife, Helen, a classy lady who stuck with me through my struggles in the 1960s and '70s with self-actualization versus caring for others. I wrestled with the angel of ambivalence, and my values wavered as I became somewhat self-absorbed. Hers never did. Her spirit of kindness and respect for others permeates whatever taste this bread leaves in your mouth, dear reader.

—RICHARD E. BYRD
Minneapolis, 1993

# * Introduction

THE NINETEENTH-CENTURY British economist Sir Walter Gilbey once said, "The employer generally gets the employee he deserves." No matter how many years go by, that statement will remain true. Whether in large corporations or small, established businesses or start-ups, the most valuable asset is the people who work there. This includes the chief executive officer as well as the individuals who buy, sell, trade, design, build, engineer, paint, and weld—those who are the heart and soul, who keep the day-to-day substance of business flowing.

Unfortunately, as society becomes more dependent on impersonal technology, the quality of business behavior has suffered. But human beings haven't changed. They still know when a kind word or phrase is sincerely meant. And they know when they are being treated with the respect and consideration that reflect their value as employees *and* as

1

human beings. Anything less only encourages cynicism and demotivates the employees we most need to perform beyond what even they believe they are capable of.

You are that employee. Your boss is that employee. Your secretary is that employee. And when you offer—and are offered—trust, respect, and consideration in your daily interactions with others, quality of life is returned to the workplace, and increased quality of life releases greater productivity and is a lot more fun as well.

The ten qualities addressed in this book offer nothing but positive benefits to those who employ them. They are symbolic derivatives of the original magic words *please* and *thank you*. First, they make the person using them as well as those on the receiving end feel good. Secondly, they are effective. They motivate people to work better. These time-honored qualities have been embraced and employed by millions of men and women for countless years. While they have, from time to time, been mistakenly discarded in the short-term quest for power or profits, we continue to return to them because they are fundamental to human relationships.

We grew up knowing that there is a difference between qualities such as trust, fairness, respect, and integrity and those of greed, bigotry, abuse, and deceit. In that case, why do so many people leave their good qualities outside the corporate door? Part of the answer lies in the way some organizations develop our bad habits. No matter how thoughtful people may ordinarily be or how they feel about the way others should be treated, they can easily fall into the bad habits present in their corporations' cultures.

The successful manager, the one who not only succeeds in his or her climb up the corporate ladder but also in life, finds a way to break those bad habits and to create an environment where trust, respect, and consideration for others grows and flourishes.

Just as we would no longer think of consciously polluting our natural environment, we as managers and employees should be conscious of keeping our corporate environments safe from pollutants like fear, selfishness, bigotry, abuse, and deceit.

As Karl Menninger says, "Worse even than ingratitude are those searing and abrasive political and administrative moves that disregard and traumatize the sentiment, the self-respect, the pride and hopes of little people, underlings and faithful workers in a system. Often it is the brashness and inconsiderateness of the action even more than the act itself. . . . To injure someone's self-respect, his pride, his status among friends and equals may be to quietly kill him."

The suggestions in this book are based on my positive experiences during the last thirty-five years as a consultant to well over a hundred large and small U.S. business and industrial corporations, professional associations, government agencies, and volunteer organizations. All of the stories related here— no matter how outrageous some of them may seem— are based on observed instances of personal affront, abuse, neglect, or insult by key supervisors, who were often unaware of the effects of their words and actions on others. Sometimes they had been treated insensitively by their own bosses and therefore felt they were justified in doing the same to others. But they often inadvertently produced undesirable results. It's as if they had somehow forgotten the simple lessons of childhood.

Of all the lessons I learned in childhood, the earliest, most useful, and most productive was to say the magic words *please* and *thank you,* words often missing from the workplace. In this book, however, I only say the magic words as a stimulus for you the reader to recall that what worked magic as a child can still work magic for you as an adult.

My hope is that this book will provide a few hints you can pass on to your boss or colleagues, or it may even help you find a flaw or two in yourself that you should attend to.

—RICHARD E. BYRD
Minneapolis

# CHAPTER ONE

*

# Trust

WHEN YOU'VE PUT your trust in someone, you generally have confidence in that person's honesty, dependability, and integrity. That person exhibits stellar qualities that help you decide to trust him, but he himself doesn't earn your trust. Trust can only be given as a gift. Once given, trust must be constantly nurtured, for it is a fragile quality and can easily be undermined through one misstep. All it takes for trust to be broken is one lie, one theft of your work, one affair.

Trust can never be taken for granted. It must be constantly renewed. If trust is broken, it is possible to reconcile and restore, depending, of course, on the severity of the break. When a trusted staff member misses a deadline, you may restore your trust in him. If he repeatedly does it, then your trust will soon be withheld. All people slip up on occasion; it is an imperfect world. That's why trust is constantly being recycled. If you find someone who offers total trust, beware. That person is too naive, an innocent lamb who is destined for an equally total shattering of his faith. Total trust should be reserved only for one's dog.

The benefits of being trusted as a manager are quite valuable. When you trust those with whom you work and they trust you in return, then the posturing and game playing that is far too prevalent in our organizations is eliminated. This certainly cuts down on suspicion, anxiety, fear, and the countless hours wasted in covering your backside.

When trust exists between you and your colleagues, then your word will be accepted as your bond, and your words will be taken at face value. You will not be seen as always strategizing and thus will not have to defend against counter-strategies. You will be given the benefit of the doubt. Your intentions will not be suspected. You will receive more latitude to accomplish your objectives. You will no longer have to suspect that the numbers presented to you have been inappropriately manipulated. You will hear bad news as well as good from those you trust. You will learn that other people care about you receiving benefit as well as they. And you will be able to make a fool of yourself on occasion without fear of long-term negative effects.

Here, then, are lessons that will help you create and nurture the quality of trust.

# LESSON #1

### If You Think They're Out to Get You, You'll Only End Up Bagging Yourself

If someone tells you they saw your subordinate having a drink with your boss after work, what do you do? Become suspicious? If a colleague whose career is on a collision course with yours is seen doing something or is quoted as saying something that seems to undermine you, do you automatically assume the worst? Or do you give people the benefit of the doubt?

Because we're all inconsistent, we say or do inappropriate things at times. We forget to send a memo to someone who should have been copied. We forget to ask someone's advice.

When you have good will on deposit with another person—what you might call money in the bank—you can make a withdrawal to cover the foible. When there is no good will present, the other person will take a countermeasure to make sure you don't repeat that action. This can become a vicious circle.

The only way to break such a circle—which occurs more often than one could possibly believe—is to start being gracious or, in other words, to always give the other person the benefit of the doubt and trust him.

When your subordinate has a private drink with your boss, you can talk to one or both, if you must, and ask if there was a result you should know about. But even that action should probably be avoided. They'll tell you if there's anything you need to know. Go to the colleague who appears to be acting to undermine you, and check out their intentions. Of course you may be lied to. You may also receive a plea of guilty to the act, although not an admission to what you had suspected.

But you may need some possible action steps when office politicians seem to be after you:

1. Be careful not to trade in your mental health and balance for a feeling of paranoia. If you consistently suspect the motives of another, then anything that person does is seen in the worst light.
2. Be your best self! Make the office politicians respond and react to you, not you to them.
3. Continually move positively toward your supposed enemies.
4. Take responsibility to change the situation or yourself. Don't whine about how others should change, or even tell others about the situation.
5. If you finally get fed up to the teeth, move on to another department or company.

One has to live nondefensively. While defenses are natural and should be developed to deal with attackers, to believe that one is always besieged leads to bizarre, distrusting, and ungracious behavior. Always give the benefit of the doubt. You can afford it. Your mental health demands it.

## LESSON #2

### The Mouse That Roars

In some companies there is what you would call the group performance appraisal, although it isn't what you may immediately suppose. It's usually negative and is designed to control or punish one or two people whom no one would personally dare to confront. A group performance appraisal would go something like this: A manager calls together his staff. He then launches forth about how they have failed him, using such terms as, "You people never do what I ask," or, "If one of you did something right, I'd have a heart attack," or, "If you people can't do the job, we'll get some new ones who will."

Such an appraisal is always ineffective. In the first place, if the entire staff quit, the manager would be in deep trouble. Second, it's parent-to-child and not adult-to-adult communication. Third, it shows that the manager's staff can get his goat.

Generally, the staff knows what the manager is doing and also knows for whom the message is intended. They just leave, shaking their heads; winning by intimidation has failed once again, and the boss loses the respect of staff members.

This may bring to mind instances at school when the teacher dressed down the entire class for the act of a few. Perhaps that's even necessary when the class won't admit to who did the dirty deed.

In this case, however, the manager knows that everyone isn't a bad performer. In their frustration, however, managers often spray their anger equally on the guilty and the innocent.

Hold your fire! Hold your temper! Cool down. Show trust in your employees' intent. If this is truly a group problem, then help the group diagnose why the problem exists. Do they really know what's expected? Do they really know how to do what's expected? Did they have the time, resources, and ability to do what's expected? What do they need from each other or from you to meet the high standards you have? In a similar situation in the future, what will they do differently? Help them learn from the experience.

If there is a culprit or two who goofed off or just acted with poor judgment, take them aside. Once again, diagnose with them what the case was. If they own up, help them plan how to work up to your expectations. Then give them support. If they won't own up, then simply make sure they understand the consequences of their behavior on you, the group, and ultimately on them if the act is repeated. No threat. Just an explanation of cause and effect.

Trust is built on your predictability, not your explosive whimsicality. It's built on belief that in the crunch you'll be there for your people. It's built on a foundation of confidence in others, not fear, inducement, and intimidation. It's a gift that can quickly be withdrawn by the giver. Negative group performance can quickly cause a withdrawal of the gift to you.

## LESSON #3

### Dig into the Problem, Not the People

One production manager had a habit of heavily criticizing presentations by his subordinates. These sessions were so tough that people who had to present to him often became physically ill. Some even threw up in the washroom ahead of time.

Tom thought he was teaching his staff to do their homework, to think through the issues, ramifications, and alternatives. But staff members felt like they were being personally abused and put on the spot and so they learned nothing except how to avoid the reviews whenever possible. Tom's questions were belittling and demeaning, often eliciting one-word responses: "Well, didn't you read Maxwell's report from last year?" or, "Don't you remember we tried that back in eighty-four?"

Tom had to learn the art of skillful questioning that would leave the staff members' self-esteem intact, even while helping them learn how to do it better the next time: "What alternatives did you consider? What did the customer ask for? Have you calculated the extra cost? Apprised the customer? What makes you think the customer will accept the new delivery date? How many shifts will you have to use to meet the schedule?" And so forth.

This session can become an interrogation, so the spirit of the session is important: You are trying to help staff members rethink the process, not simply raise hell. Have they covered all the bases, thought through what could happen? You want your staff members to become more and more effective at thinking so that each new problem, no matter how complex, will be tackled appropriately. At the same time, on this particular project you still want the best answer.

The most effective way good managers have of bringing about change is by asking questions that cause staff members to rethink the issue. So dig into the problem but not the people. Get the best answer—together.

## LESSON #4

### Overkill

President Teddy Roosevelt once said that the man who starts a fight admits he's lost the argument. In the same way, managers who resort to the ultimate weapon of threatening job replacement admit they can no longer manage.

You've probably heard of a manager who has said (usually shouted), "If you don't do what I've asked, I'll get someone who can." This phrase is often used in front of the person's peers. Sometimes it's used by a boss who says it bravely to his whole staff at once. "If you people can't turn these production problems around, then I'll get some people who can."

Of course, the expression has several sources and intended consequences. Its source may be complete frustration on the manager's part that a bad situation doesn't seem amenable to change. It may also be a deliberate attempt to frighten the staff into extraordinary attempts to achieve what the manager wants.

There may be a time for threats, although they should certainly be used sparingly because of the unintended consequences that always occur. For example, people under threat hide and do not trust. Once the threat of this ultimate weapon has been brandished:

1. The manager is now viewed by staff as unable to control himself.
2. The staff takes the manager seriously. Therefore, they stop telling that person anything that would trigger such threats.
3. The staff members who have self-respect and mobility begin planning to bail out of this group.
4. The staff will get uptight and less able to perform in the creative ways needed to solve the problem.
5. The staff who remain with the boss over a reasonable period may feel diminished, less confident, and increasingly powerless. The result is poorer performance in the long run.

To paraphrase another of Teddy's sayings: You've got the big stick; you can afford to speak softly—and consistently. That's the way trust is formed and maintained. Threats are a threat to trust.

## LESSON #5

### Stand by Your Man

Recently, Bill, a supervisor of new sales recruits, got approval from his boss to install a test that would help develop the profiles of successful employees. The company psychologist approved and cooperated with the test. However, although Bill was unaware of it, his boss's boss was opposed to testing of any kind.

Bill was notified to report to the office of the "big" boss. He entered the room and noted that his boss was there, too. The big boss excoriated him for attempting to make company policy, accepted nothing he said in his own defense, and then dismissed him. Bill's boss, though present, said nothing.

Bill's boss could have said, "I really approved of this new test and the project. Bill did not act unilaterally." Or he could have said to his boss, "Could I speak to you privately for a moment before we talk to Bill?" and then he could have told his boss that he'd approved the project. That would have saved Bill from embarrassment, with its bad results, and saved the big boss from having egg on his face for not properly gathering information.

Obviously, the big boss was out of line to handle the situation in that fashion, but Bill's boss didn't do well, either. He should have at least tried to prevent the meeting with the big boss from taking place.

If he could not have done so, he should have put himself on the line during the meeting. Failing to do so created a circumstance that made Bill hesitate to ever trust his boss again.

Bill had done what he thought was appropriate, with what he thought was the approval of his boss. Bill had acted responsibly, his boss irresponsibly. By failing to stand by his man, he acted cowardly. Fess up when you helped create the problem or risk losing your employees' trust forever. Once bitten, more than twice shy.

## LESSON #6

### Manipulation, the Enemy of Trust

One senior manager in a large government agency liked to keep underlings standing in front of his desk while he finished something. As staff members stood there, fantasies of doing the manager bodily harm would flash through their minds. An administrator of a large urban hospital always demanded that his underlings stand on one foot when they came to see him "in order to keep meetings short." Another manager removed all the chairs except his own from his office to discourage visitors from lingering longer than absolutely necessary.

Many of us have talked to a colleague who wanted help in deliberately intimidating a vendor, a customer, or the head of another unit. Some managers encourage winning through intimidation and have given permission to their staffs to use such techniques.

Deliberate intimidation taps into fear as a primary motivator. While it's true that fear does motivate, it never produces the kind of long-term results one really desires. For example, if you make it an uncomfortable or demeaning experience to talk to you, people will soon find ways to avoid seeing you. If you threaten a customer by saying, "If you don't buy this new line, you won't get any parts for your old machines," you're asking the customer to find another supplier. With manipulation and intimidation, you are sending strong signals that you do not find others fully human, that they are in some way not to be trusted.

If you treat people as objects, they'll return the favor. If you treat them as people, you'll find they reciprocate. Out of such a relationship, one that does not rely on manipulation or intimidation, can come trust. And out of such trust can come the kind of performance that every manager wants from a staff.

### LESSON #7

#### Micromanaging

Micromanagement comes in many forms. Sometimes it appears in the boss's need to know where you are at all times or triple-check the numbers you've given him. Sometimes the boss gives the same job to three different people to "make sure it gets done." Creating over-reporting methods and demanding that your staff know everything all the time, whenever asked, creates a low-trust environment that makes the other people feel smothered and enfeebled.

One boss constantly peeked at the work on her subordinate's desk, going through folders. She would never think to apologize because her style was to manage the detail of her employee's work. How could she know what to manage if she didn't get the details? The micromanager dips two or three levels below to give orders, bypassing the supervisory structure. The micromanager never takes anything at face value, which by definition means not trusting associates.

One manager, who finally got a boss who didn't micromanage, said, "For thirty years I spent my days preparing reports of data, just in case my boss asked for them. Now I finally have time to actually manage my department."

Obviously, a great manager keeps his eye on the detail because that's where you often get "killed." But if you bypass the people who are your direct reports, demand complete backup for every figure, and expect your direct reports to have whatever you want to know at their fingertips, you should fire them, manage their functions, and save the company lots of money.

## LESSON #8

### Stop Enjoying Yourselves! Why Do You Think It's Called Work?

Some years ago, a group of managers was touring a plant that belonged to their company. Such touring was unusual, but so was this plant. The plant handled a complicated photographic process that involved 500 people, toxic chemicals, expensive film, and other sensitive raw materials.

Over a five-year period, this plant had eliminated all management but the plant manager. At the same time, manufacturing costs per unit were down dramatically. Waste was practically nonexistent. Schedules were met. Teams measured and managed themselves and their processes. Very impressive.

The tour group was taken through the plant. Two of the touring vice presidents noticed a couple of employees who were off to the side talking and laughing. The vice presidents suspected this pair was wasting time rather than working.

Some managers believe that "idle hands are the devil's tools." Anyone who understands manufacturing, however, knows that there are times when certain people are better off doing nothing than they are doing more of what's not needed and what jams the line. Anyone who really believes in results would not criticize people for talking or laughing if the results were there.

Many managers suspect that most people, given

the freedom, will goof off, take too many unwarranted sick days, or take advantage of the company in some other way. Unfortunately, some will, but they get much more press than they deserve.

In this plant the results were there. Expectations were being exceeded, and people needed to be admired, not suspected.

Watch your suspicions, for suspicions breed further distrust. And that distrust can lead employees to be dissatisfied with their jobs, which in turn can produce the goofing off you wanted to stop in the first place.

## LESSON #9

### Need-to-Know Versus Nice-to-Know

Tom told his newly formed staff, "You can count on me to keep you informed, but purely on a need-to-know basis. We're all too busy to bother with nice-to-know information." As the staff filed out, Mary said to Bob, "I think we should treat him the same. Let's just tell him what *we* think *he* needs to know!"

This vignette suggests possible disaster. The boss doesn't want that much screening of information going on. Obviously, Mary and Bob can't feel included if the boss will only tell them what he thinks they need to know. Most of the rich fabric of information out of which the best work is done is of the nice-to-know variety. Tom has indicated he's going to control the information flow and decide what is relevant.

Trust is constantly fed by a free flow of information and feelings between the relevant people. When a boss overmanages information, the exchange of data becomes the coinage of power rather than the basis for trust.

You don't have the time to pass on everything you hear. Still, with the exceptions of breaking SEC rules, personal confidences, and gossip, you should keep your people informed of factors that may have an impact on their work; share your observations and value judgments about customers, organization changes, and aspirations; and ask for feedback on how you are communicating.

It's always better to include and inform more than necessary, rather than not enough. That way you make people not only feel they are on the inside, but that you actually put them there.

## LESSON #10

### Nothing Personal

Here's a common scenario: A manager walks into the office of one of his direct reports, let's call him George. He enters without knocking (of course) to discuss an item that is of major importance to him. He's thwarted because George is talking on the telephone. He stands impatiently, making sure he is in full view of George, waiting for the call to end. He's able to hear only one side of the phone conversation, which goes like this: "You're kidding! You just gotta be kidding, aren't you?! (ha ha) I can't imagine that!

Not me. I wouldn't have even asked the guy to go! (pause) No, I just wouldn't! (pause) What?! He got a red one? My god!"

It's obvious that this is a personal phone call, and it's taking up the manager's precious time. He begins shifting his weight from one foot to another, pacing back and forth across the room looking at his watch. He debates about leaving a caustic note for George, telling him to see him when he's through with his "important call." He fantasizes about just ordering George to cradle the damn phone so he can talk with him. Maybe he actually says, "George, hang up! I have an important item to discuss. Call back later!" Or maybe he decides to really punish George for not being sensitive to his presence and the importance of his mission, so he turns on his heel and leaves, shutting the door more noisily than is necessary.

A few minutes later, George calls on his boss. He's obviously aware that the executive is upset. He's nervous and defensive, or deferential, or feeling some way that takes energy away from doing his job.

George then tells his boss that he has been on the phone with Tom Jacobs, who happens to be a vice president at one of the company's biggest clients. After placing the largest order that the firm has ever made, he told George an amusing story about a friend who had just purchased a red Ferrari.

Suddenly, the manager's "major" issue is no longer major in his mind. He realizes that the "personal" conversation he had overhead was simply polite good fellowship, the appreciative sharing of a story that came after a deal's close—a deal that will allow his department to exceed its annual goal four months early.

Chances are that the manager felt rather foolish, if not lousy. And he may even have vowed in the future to think the best of the other person, until proven differently. This kind of attitude is always the best way to motivate others, since people are likely to live up, or down, to the expectations you set for them.

# CHAPTER TWO

\*

# Fairness

THE QUALITY OF fairness is one everyone is taught in kindergarten. When Joey wants all the toys in the sandbox, the teacher intervenes to divide the toys equally between Joey and you, urging Joey to be fair. She treats you and Joey alike, without reference to whether she likes Joey better than you. The quality is reflected in words like impartial, unbiased, and evenhanded.

From kindergarten through old age, the issue of fairness plagues us. As a manager, you are constantly faced with it: When hiring, people resent the boss's son getting a job; when promoting, old boy networks are feared; when giving performance-based raises, no one is happy; and when doing compensation, fairness is sought through market comparison on a job.

Managers all face the criticism that they have unfair perks, such as private, close-to-the-building parking places, and, of course, they give too much work to one person and not enough to another.

However fair you may feel you are, in someone's eyes you'll be unfair. To seek fairness is required. To be perceived as fair is illusive. Is it fair to give a minority person an advantage, all else being equal? Is it fair for you to have the corner office with lovely furniture when you're never there, while your secretary has an inside cubicle where she has to work all day long? Is it fair for you to let the single mother in your unit take more sick time than the others who have no children? Is it fair for you to give the person who is a quick study more work than the slower colleague? Yes and no, depending on how and by whom it is perceived and on what criteria.

Of course you try to reward people on a principle of fairness and equitable treatment, but life itself seems unjust to many. Do, in fact, "the good die young?" If so, why?

Whether or not it's achieved or perceived, fairness must continue to be your goal. It's giving others their due. It's entering a fight in the office to keep it fair, even though you may get bloodied. It's doing the right thing by your own lights as you listen to the many protestations of others. It's being able to like the face you see in the mirror at the end of the day.

In the final analysis, people will accept your actions even if they disagree with you, as long as they believe you acted out of the principle of fairness. When people believe you seek to be fair, they will carry out the decision with enthusiasm. They'll focus on the task to be accomplished rather than spending half their working time worrying about whether they should be looking out for themselves and their self-interest.

It's likely that a fair boss can prevent the formation of competitive, informal networks based upon resentment. Such groups create unions when the bosses aren't perceived as fair. Other groups undermine good products coming to market because of personal vendettas rather than for objective reasons.

Here are some lessons that may help you as you seek to be fair.

## LESSON #11

### There's No Such Thing as a Perfect Translation

TOM: Gawd, I couldn't believe how funny you must have appeared at that staff meeting.

BILL: What do you mean? Did someone tell you something?

TOM: Yes, Mary told me she just couldn't believe the way you were set up at that meeting.

BILL: Really? I guess I didn't realize that!

On the surface, it appears to be an innocuous conversation. What possible harm could it do to tell Bill about what Mary said about him? Then again, what possible good could it do? Just who is being helped by repeating a staff member's shared feelings or thoughts about a coworker, even if they are apparently noncontroversial comments?

It simply isn't fair for you to report to a person what another has said about him. You can't repeat the comment within the context or with the tone of voice or nonverbal expression the other person had. So, whatever the comment, it will not be what was originally communicated to you. When you try to represent another's comment, you are not fair to the person who said it because they may not have wanted it repeated, or they may have wanted the opportunity to express themselves to the person you've told. The very fact that you had a private conversation that you reported could appear quite unfair to the person you are telling.

You are also being unfair to yourself. You may end up being seen as a gossip at best and intentionally destructive at worst. In other words, your reasons for repeating the third party's comments will be suspect. Perhaps you did just see it as funny. But you are putting the person you are telling in a difficult situation. Should Bill confront Mary? Should he be wary? What should he do with this gratuitous report?

More often than not, we pass on these conversations for our own ends, which we may not even be acknowledging to ourselves. For example, do you want to undermine the relationship of the parties involved, or to show yourself as the loyal one, or impress the other person that you are someone's confidant, or hurt the person you're telling without being held responsible?

"But," you protest, "my intentions are honorable. I'm simply trying to help two people understand each other a little better." If that's so, you must repeat the tone of voice, the nuances, the body language, and the exact words. Even then, you can't really represent the person you're quoting.

If you think your confidant should actually talk to the other person, help that happen. Generally, people can represent themselves better and more fairly than you or anyone else can.

## LESSON #12

### Sexual Bullying

The factory supervisor in *Les Miserables*, the classic French morality story, fires Fantine because, unlike the other factory women, she rejects his sexual advances. He reasons that since she has had a child out of wedlock, she has no right to act as if she were virtuous.

A theme common to all world literature is the story of obvious unfairness, where, for fear of losing their security, women have had to trade their sexual favors to men who had the power to take away that security. While one can point to instances as old as Joseph and Potiphar's wife in Genesis where women have done the same, clearly men, who more often control job security, have overtly, and without real affection, forced women to accept their sexual advances for the sake of job security.

In the workplace, there are always sexual dynamics that confound the best intentions. Both men and women get caught up in the tangle of natural and unnatural emotions. That this will continue, no one can doubt. As women continue to pursue careers and not just jobs to help their families, they become colleagues and competitors with men and office dynamics become more complex. Stories will abound of seduction, sexual harassment, love affairs, broken marriages, and forced sex. Charges and counter-charges will fly. New relationships will form and old ones will be destroyed.

But even in all the confusion, male—and female—managers can restrain themselves from forcing someone who works for them into tolerating sexual bullying in order to hold a job. In the modern world, it is illegal. It has always been unfair.

Also, in the modern world, with women in positions of power over men, an admonition against sexual bullying no longer applies to just one gender. For such behavior is not only about sex, it is also about power. And abuse of power can be wielded by a woman as well as a man. To take sexual advantage of subordinates, then, simply because one has the power to see them fired, is one of the more abusive—and unfair—uses of power.

## LESSON #13

### Busy Signals

As we all know, one of the worst and most needless time-wasters is telephone tag. The usual responses when you return someone's call are, "He's not at his desk," "She's in a meeting," or even, "He's busy. Could he call you later?" And yet, more often than not, the message left for you was that the caller was anxious to talk to you.

The options for you, of course, are quite simple. You can inform your secretary that you are expecting a return call, say where you'll be, and include instructions to have you summoned from a meeting or paged. If you can't or won't take a return call, then make it clear you will call later, and offer some times.

If you're the person returning the call, be sure to tell the person answering the phone that you were requested to call. If that person says the boss can't be interrupted, you can say, "I understand and sympathize. Please have him call," or, "Would you please put a note in front of him saying I'm on the phone?" Many times the person in between doesn't know what to do, not having been given instructions. You need to help, because after a while, people get tired of trying to return a call to a person who never seems to be available to receive it.

If you call someone, make yourself available for the return call. It isn't fair to expect the person being called to continue to pursue you when it's your nickel in the first place.


## LESSON #14

### Think Before You Speak

One manager, returning from a lengthy trip, turned on his computer to find an updated word processing program installed. He was irritated because

he was just getting used to the old computer program.
He announced his irritation very loudly for all to hear
and then asked that the old program be reinstalled.
He later learned that the programmer's feelings had
been hurt. She'd worked hard installing the new and
more useful program as a surprise. While publicly
verbalizing his anger and frustration, he had not
calculated the impact of his words on her.

Once you become a manager, you take on certain
surrogate parental, but not maternal or paternal,
characteristics for most younger people. The manager is not just anyone, but rather the one who
giveth and taketh away self-esteem, raises, promotions, and exciting assignments. The manager who
does not realize that his words or lack of words at
certain times have larger-than-life consequences is
a dangerous missile without a sensor system. Even
when frustrated, assume the good intentions of those
around you. Such an assumption will lead you to discover not only what really happened, but also why.

## LESSON #15

### Mountains Out of Molehills

One manger had the habit of dipping deep into
his organization when he'd find one small number
that happened to be recorded in error. He turned
this into a cause célèbre and suggested to his staff
that he no longer could believe any of their numbers.
They, of course, felt this kind of generalization was
unfair, presenting them as incompetent or devious

and their boss as the only person truly watching the store.

Another manager would wander around the organization until he found some small problem such as one testing device that was letting through products that would later be found to be unshippable. And while the matter clearly needed attention, he berated the production crew in his next column in the company newsletter—this, while attempting to have the work force positively motivated to produce a product that was already nearly perfect.

The manager should give attention to detail. Detail is often where the game is lost or gained, but to make small matters into gigantic issues may signal people to work on the wrong priorities. In other words, they may become so frightened of making small mistakes that they lose the larger picture. They may, for example, grind up resources with excessively redundant systems.

Don't unfairly jump to conclusions or rush to judgment until you see a pattern of mistakes develop. Focusing on single errors and generalizing will, at a very minimum, violate a sense of fair play, especially with good performers.

## LESSON #16

### And It's Right, Too!

One human resource vice president took the time to carefully develop a document on how and why a policy of hiring and promoting a diverse work force would be profitable and reasonable for the company. He indicated that the available neighborhood employee pool was increasingly made up of people of color and that something other than an all-white management team would be needed to motivate and direct this work force. He also indicated that they would be in better compliance with government requirements and thus would prevent possible loss of contracts. Further, he suggested, class action suits had become increasingly popular as an option to eliminating systematic discrimination and their company was a possible target, given their past and current practices. Finally, he suggested that the customer base was also becoming more diverse, and a diverse work force was likely to create an advantage for the company over their competitors, who were not making such efforts.

The senior executive who had reviewed the document returned the paper with an attached memo that said, "Good argument. It's *right* and *fair,* too!" While this manager was logical and analytical, she also managed by having a core of values that guided her decision making. Being right and fair were strong parts of her character. She never apologized for them.

You as a manager may prevent customers from being cheated unfairly even when it can be done without being caught. You as a manager can treat employees fairly who perform well but who are not liked. You as a manager can make sure that the safety of your product is never questionable, that your products do what your ads claim, and that your competitive practices aren't illegal—all because it's right and fair.

## LESSON #17

### To Be Fair, Treat People Unequally

John was permitted to leave for three days for the funeral of his father, while Mary was not. John's religion required it. Mary's did not. But was that fair? On the other hand, Mary had been putting in a lot of travel time for the company. Although company policy prevented her from going first class, her boss told her he wanted her to do it for the near future until they reviewed how much travel was really being required of her. He recognized her stress. But was that fair to others who also had to travel?

One major reason for organization policies is to assure employees that the company will be evenhanded with everyone so that playing favorites is harder for supervisors to do. Max Weber, the supposed inventor of bureaucracy, really had fairness in mind when he advocated job parity, equal treatment for equal pay, and the elimination of preferential treatment for salary, perks, and other benefits, based upon the boss's whims and exploitation of the vulnerable by management. Union work rules also came into being because originally companies did not fairly compensate people for their contributions.

The administration of policy, however, is rarely fair. The reason for this is that people's needs are so different that almost each case is an exception. This is true both of customers and employees.

Therefore, in what can be considered a paradox, in order to be fair, people should be treated unequally. Judges face the issue every day as they administer sentences using sentencing guidelines. Justice (or fairness) must always take into account the individual's contribution, stress level, loyalty, commitment, religious beliefs, cultural expectations, and personal sensitivities.

Of course, being fair becomes a nightmare for you as you move from rule-based policies to more need-based applications. But you really have no choice when the work force includes people sharing jobs, single parents providing high talent, and people from different cultural traditions. Each manager finds it an obligation to make the rules fit the person, not the reverse. To do otherwise is to violate the quality of fairness.

## LESSON #18

### "She Services the Managers"

Charlie welcomed the two new male managers to his staff meeting. He asked all the male managers to introduce themselves and to tell the new men what their responsibilities were. While this began to happen, jokes began to fly and humorous comments about each other's experiences were shared. The atmosphere was one of give-and-take locker room humor. Then Charlie introduced his human resource manager by saying, "I'd also like you to meet Jane, more affectionately known as Tarzan's

mate, who services the managers." Loud guffaws
followed as a couple of the managers reminded
her of the location of their offices. Jane smiled,
but inside she was pained at the presumption of
intimacy, especially with the two new managers.

After the meeting, Jane went to Charlie's office
to tell him she thought his remark had been out of
line. Charlie said, "Hey, it was all in fun," which
was what he always said after such gaffes. Jane
sighed, looked at his crestfallen expression, and
said, "Please, Charlie, just be a little sensitive
to my feelings." As Jane left, Charlie said to
himself, "She sure can be bitchy and narrow-
minded."

No one wins in this situation. Charlie becomes
wary of Jane and resents not being able to "have
fun." The new managers were embarrassed at the
rough humor. The old managers just see one more
instance of Charlie's insensitivity.

Humor, when laced with sexual innuendo, is questionable at all times, in public, in front of strangers, at the expense of a woman in a group of men,
because it presumes an intimacy that may not be
there, and because it corners the person in such a
way that to complain means being a bad sport. It
isn't fair.

Most male groups share sexually explicit jokes,
comments, and stories of sexual prowess. It's not
fair to make the price of admission for a woman
to be the ever-present butt of those jokes and comments. Some women may not be bothered and may
like the attention. Most don't, even if they won't
admit it.

Nor is it fair when women in a predominantly female organization make snide remarks about the male secretary's estrogen levels or another male's prowess in the boudoir.

No matter what your sex, as a manager you must always be aware of treating those who work for you in a manner that demonstrates you are not taking unfair advantage of them.

## LESSON #19

### The Pawn Brokers

We'd be rich if we had a nickel for every time we've seen positions changed by senior management without adequate communication to the person who's being moved, to the people who are suddenly the person's new bosses, or even to the person whose function the new enrollee will replace. The employee may well say, "It just isn't fair!"

Sometimes people hear by the grapevine that they're being moved out of their jobs. They may have their reporting relationships downgraded without being told why. They may be transferred to a new division or function without explanation. They may hear from colleagues about a promotion they're going to receive before they've even been approached.

The thoughtless things done to people in the name of expedience or lack of time are legendary and leave the person affected feeling like an interchangeable part of a machine. They may be twenty-year employees; that doesn't seem to matter. A person's rights when his career is at stake must be considered. He has a right to have some input in the change. He has a right to say no without jeopardizing his job. He has a right to be treated fairly.

As China's ancient Tao puts it, "Don't do to others what you wouldn't want done to you." How quickly we can profoundly violate a sense of fair play by thoughtlessly manipulating people as if they were only pawns at a corporate chess board.

## LESSON #20

### Who Called This Meeting Anyway?

When a child comes to a parent for some advice, the parent offers up his words of wisdom. Sometimes, though, the parent doesn't stop there, seeing an opportunity to advise on other matters that have been on the parent's mind. Soon the child realizes that a simple question is more likely to get an encyclopedic response, and avoids asking altogether. Bosses, unfortunately, can have the same effect on their staff.

As a manager, you probably have stored up at least five things you need to say to your staff members, and there never seems to be time to get to them. But when staff members have made appointments to talk with you about their own concerns, that's not the time to dig out your agenda.

If a meeting has been called by another person, then it's that person's problem that has to be addressed. Of course, how it's worked on is another matter. There are some managers who are my-story's-worse-than-your-story bosses. A staff member who comes to them with a serious concern, looking for coaching or at least a friendly ear, ends up getting, "Let me tell you about my situation," followed by a thirty-minute dissertation on the boss's problems. What the staff member then thinks, of course, is, "Who needs this? I'll figure it out myself."

As a manager, you need to know what's going on in your organization, and the best way to know is to be perceived and used as a coach. When direct reports seek advice in a meeting they've called, then:

1. Listen, and help define the problem.
2. Listen, and help them develop alternative approaches.
3. Listen, and help them evaluate those options.
4. Listen, and applaud their selected alternatives.
5. Listen, and offer to meet with them to evaluate whether their choice worked.

You have the right to call meetings whenever you want to, to talk about whatever you want. Your staff person may well feel that it's hard to get time with you. It's not then fair of you to use the time he's requested for your purposes. He will leave feeling quite empty and resentful that you ate up what he considered his time.

If you want to see a staff member about an issue that concerns you, then you call a meeting.

## LESSON #21

### Near Fatal Attractions

If you have made a personal connection with the lust or love of your life under your supervision, beware.

First of all, the nature of the relationship is almost always public knowledge. The flowers, candy, intimate glances, quiet lunches, trips together to customers "because we're a good team," are all observable and duly noted.

If you both are married (to different people), that bothers your colleagues. If only one of you is married, that, too, bothers your colleagues. Even when you both are single, it's troublesome. When the two of you get into personal spats that can be heard from behind closed doors, it's embarrassing to everyone. You aren't then doing the object of your affection any good at all. He or she will become the "fall guy" when, not generally *if,* the whole matter gets raised to higher authorities. And that's unfair to him or her, as the case may be.

In addition to making the staff member an object of ridicule and embarrassment, you can't be certain, ever, how much your power over their job security plays a part in their "attraction." As the other person's boss, your love may, especially if younger, be reacting to being flattered by the attention of you, the older, wiser, prestigious boss. That's an unfair advantage, even if you aren't intentionally using your position.

If you find yourself beginning to cast seductive glances toward one of your staff members, or they toward you, put an end to it. Talk to the person directly about what problems the acting out of feelings can produce. Depending on how strong the infatuation, for your career's sake, your staff member's sake, and for the sake of every colleague, stop the flirtation or transfer one of you to different units.

It's true that some romantic relationships between bosses and staff members have flowered into long-term successes. Many have not. In either case, people can suffer from the effects of these affairs. If you find yourself in this situation, ask yourself, "Am I being fair to all concerned?" If the answer is no, or you find yourself straining to make your answer fit your desires, then take the matter up with a counselor you can trust.

# CHAPTER THREE

## *

# Generosity

ONE MIGHT THINK that the quality of generosity is quite out of place in business. Nothing could be farther from the truth. Charles Dickens's *A Christmas Carol* presents a miserly Scrooge whose stingy business practices extend to his private life. The story is famous because we admire a person who is generous both personally and in business.

In business practices, this quality becomes evident in those who seek fair negotiation and not simply the advantage. Always seeking the advantage and using whatever leverage you have to get it creates suspicion that may well make others wait quietly until they can get the upper hand.

With customers, generosity is providing better service or products than is expected, and always more than required. It's the guarantee that is unqualified, not because the customer is always right or honest but because you practice generosity as part of your business ethic.

With colleagues, generosity is forgiving past griev-
ances even when there is no overt apology. It's open-
ly praising the competition when they win and not
crowing publicly when you beat them, no matter
how elated you are and how tempting it may be.
It's also being more likely to speak positively of
colleagues when they aren't present, or at least not
to comment at all, as your parents probably admon-
ished you when you were young.

With your staff, generosity means always giving
them the benefit of the doubt when rumors fly or
appearances indicate something awry. It means
pushing them, but praising them when they do
something well. It means giving them the credit,
never taking it for yourself. It means providing
opportunities for them to shine in presentations,
customer contacts, or tasks that seem beyond their
immediate capacity.

Generous managers also seek ways to serve the
less fortunate with their time and money. Sometimes it's in the community; sometimes it's within
their own work force.

A generous manager speaks more often of *we* than
of *I* when extolling the organization's accomplishments. Above all, the generous manager accepts people from different backgrounds, cultures, or beliefs
for what and who they are. People know that this
manager will fill in the empty spots in his picture of
them with positive assumptions, not negative suspicions.

As a manager you have to realize, from a very
practical point of view, that life and business are
not a series of transactions. Memories are long. Your

reputation precedes you. Those you cheat or fail to be openhanded with today will have their turn someday. If advantage is all you seek, then you'll be more likely to create relationships, both personal and business, where the other person will do the same. In other words, this quality of generosity is just good business, if nothing else.

These lessons show some ways that generosity can help you really connect with your business associates, with results that will be productive for your business and your life.

## LESSON #22

### When the *I*'s Shouldn't Have It

Everyone knows a manager who assumes that one of the perks of the position is being allowed the peculiar habit of using the first person singular when describing his unit's accomplishments, even though it's obvious to everyone that those accomplishments were the result of a team effort.

Beginning every sentence with *I* is on the increase, especially when companies merge, reorganize, or downsize. In these circumstances many people begin thinking how they can look good. And there are those who don't need an excuse for thinking in the first person singular. For them, every subject, every bit of news is seen through a prism of, "So, what does it mean to me?" A manager of a large computer company once sent a subordinate in her place to a meeting with her boss. When the subordinate returned, the first question the manager asked had nothing to do with the topic of the meeting. What she wanted to know, first and foremost, was, "Did they talk about me?" Most people are suspicious of such narcissism. Indeed, superiors may see it as career-limiting behavior.

The worst slight is when the people who did the work are not allowed to put their name on the product or to present the result of their work. It seems almost like stealing to the staff person when superiors put their names exclusively on work they did not produce.

In one organization that represented the United States in a foreign country, the boss reviewed, changed, and signed every report and piece of correspondence, often holding up progress immeasurably. The fact that only his name appeared on anything that went out resulted in scores of professionals having no written connection with their foreign counterparts.

If you and your staff members made something happen and your own contribution has indeed been overwhelming, let someone else recognize it. While false modesty is exactly that, false, your generosity permits others to appreciate themselves as well as to appreciate you.

## LESSON #23

### Symbolic Gestures

While we know that clothes do not really make the man or woman, in many organizations they still signal how serious a person is in making advances in a company. In one corporation it is considered too flamboyant for men to wear loafers with tassels. In another it shows an acceptable sense of style. In one *Fortune* 500 company a new hire from England left a bad impression by wearing a blue dress shirt with a white collar. In some firms a woman in a suit is a woman on the way up. In other companies female managers are encouraged to wear dresses.

Some corporate dress codes' unwritten rules—and most are unwritten—appear a bit silly, yet, if not followed, they can seriously hinder a person's advancement. In one financial services organization, a very fine operations supervisor was seeking promotion. He'd prided himself on his independence in a very positive but blue pinstripe suit environment. His people wore short sleeves on all occasions. So did he. It was a small thing, but a small thing is sometimes the key to a large door. His colleagues saw this practice as acceptable, but acceptable only for someone working in the back room. They liked him but didn't really believe he was an equal member of their management group.

His boss recognized that there were other factors involved in John's career movement, or lack thereof, but he knew that the sleeves were a symbol to others that, in fact, affected his receptiveness. It therefore needed to be dealt with. So he brought John in and said, "I know this is personal. You can tell me it's none of my business, but at least listen, please." He proceeded to talk about what the short sleeves indicated to others. He said he hoped John would at least consider what dressing differently might communicate.

John was very pleased to have the boss take such interest. He might not have been, and he might have felt justified in telling the boss that his manner of dress was his own business. His boss, however, thought it necessary for John to understand the impact of his behavior but to allow him to make his choice.

Feedback that is unsolicited is always given at some risk to the giver. To offer feedback, knowing that your gift as well as the attendant risk might actually alienate the other person is, from one point of view, an act of generosity where the hand that feeds can get bitten.

## LESSON #24

### Back Scratching

The expression *back scratching* has such a manipulative connotation. It implies the intent to get something in return for giving something. A generous manager, however, gives without expecting something in return.

Some years ago a manager from a defense company told this story: A colleague of his came out of a Pentagon meeting where he had heard a discussion that would surely have an impact on the success of the manager's program. Before boarding his plane for the return trip, he telephoned the manager to tell him what he heard at the meeting. The manager was not at all surprised his colleague had called him. The man had a reputation for looking out for the success of others in the company, not just his own.

You can see such generosity in other areas. For example, the true nature of professional golf comes through when the winner gives credit to another who has helped him immensely with his game, even during the tournament in which they were competing.

True generosity is helping colleagues to do their best, even when the immediate result may not be to your benefit. Winners can afford to do it. And you're already a winner just by doing it.

## LESSON #25

### The End Run

As often happens, two divisions in a company may be working for the same customer. When that customer requests a product or service that appears to be a simple extension of the divisions' offerings, it's only normal that both divisions will pursue the business.

In one particular case, one division of a company had the charter to create control systems for airplanes. The other had the same mission for rockets. As time went on, one of their customers began to create airplane designs that had no live pilot and were used as target drones or even as missiles. The other division had a customer who was creating manned rockets. The question became, What was an airplane and what was a rocket?

In another situation, a tool division of a company charged with making components began upgrading their tools with electronics that were mini-systems. A sister division with a systems charter was responding to their customer's needs to develop less costly small system tools. The first division's customer was usually the director of engineering. The second division sold the president on their systems. Both could serve different customers in the same client organization. Now, however, the question became, When did a component become a system and thus a charter to be violated?

In both cases, the marketing group of one division made a pitch to their group vice presidents to expand their charter to grab the initiative in the emerging market. While initiative might be applauded, in both cases the other division was not notified that this end run was taking place. While seeking to get an advantage on the other divisions by influencing the group vice presidents, they created serious rifts in personal relationships with their sister divisions. They had engineered a "grab," which the group vice presidents saw through, and alienated friends and colleagues who just couldn't believe such self-serving behavior. The divisions making the end runs were, of course, concerned about saving or increasing jobs and market expansion. They miscalculated, however, for the downside of such behavior damaged the next proposed partnerships with their sister divisions.

When a charter needs changing, go to the sister division and work out a common proposal to present to your group vice president. In that fashion you can control your own destiny, maintain long-term relationships, and do what's best for the company. That's generosity and openhandedness at its best!

## LESSON #26

### Forget Moderation, Excess Works!

Highly successful managers go the extra mile with their colleagues, especially with their direct reports. It is not unlike the satisfaction customers feel when they know a special effort was made on their behalf. Your direct reports know you care when you unselfishly lavish your time to make them successful. Here are some of the ways highly successful managers go the extra mile:

1. They attend the bar mitzvahs, baptisms, weddings, and graduations of their direct reports.
2. If possible, they show up at the funerals of their direct reports and of their spouses or parents.
3. They participate in interventions with the family, friends, and coworkers to stop a direct report's

misuse of alcohol or drugs. They hold the strongest card by holding the power to separate the person from his job. One senior manager would jump on a plane to confront a valued manager a thousand miles away. Nothing was too much for his guys.

4. When direct reports have emergencies, their managers provide cars, planes, doctors, or whatever is necessary. The cost will be negligible compared to the appreciation of the affected direct report.

5. They permit—even encourage—calls at home when in the best judgment of their direct report it is for the well-being of the company.

6. If a direct report doesn't seem to be performing, they first assume they are being a poor coach. They help him succeed with all their resources, on company or personal time.

7. If they find they can't understand what a direct report is saying is the reason for his problem, they spend a day on-site shadowing him.

These are but a few of the excesses that make for highly successful people managers. Whatever you choose to do, do it in excess. Such generosity and sacrifice will be rewarded.

## LESSON #27

### Take the First Step

When a conflict develops between two managers,
as it often does, some very poor behavior may result.
Usually the issue is one of control. Who's going to
win the argument? Who's going to back down and
thus lose face? Who's going to take the first step
toward reconciliation?

You've seen the paper trail of such disputes, the
memos flying back and forth, complete with barbs
both business and personal: "You'd have understood
my point if you'd been listening and not simply trying to figure out ways to destroy and discredit my
proposal," or, "Don't do me any favors by coming to
any more of my program reviews. With help like
yours, we can soon forget about being in this market."

Whether oral or written, such barbs become the
stuff of rumor and attention, often causing others
to have to line up behind one or the other on the
basis of loyalty rather than substance. Often their
boss doesn't know what to do except exhort both parties to behave differently, or tell them to cease and
desist, which may drive the dispute underground, or
perhaps decide in favor of one or the other, which
never really settles the dispute.

Before the boss is forced to intercede, often with
less than adequate results, a generous manager will
take steps. While not wanting to lose the argument,

he still wants to resolve the dispute. He realizes that by *moving against* the other manager through memos and other means, he is confronting and escalating the dispute. By *moving away,* the result may be that he is seen as copping out or as causing a stalemate on the substantive issue.

Rather, a manager with a generous spirit should *move toward* the other party to de-escalate feelings in order to regain a reasonable relationship. Only when this is done can a solution to the substantive issue be achieved. Such a movement takes courage.

So be the first to put out your hand. Be the second to put out your hand. When you are twice rejected, go to others to help you put out your hand. Always remain prepared to put out your hand in conciliation. What you should be seeking is the truth of a situation, not the advantage over a colleague. It's the only way to get back to business.

## LESSON #28

### One Hundred Ten Percent Certainty

At some developmental point in life, a few people find that the way to be successful is to always express themselves with absolute certainty. They may not always be right, but they're never in doubt. In a debate, or even in a program or product review, it's a great way to position yourself. It forces others to really think through their position and to clearly define their disagreements with you. A good exchange can then take place, and if the other people's arguments are strong, you may have to concede certain points.

Unfortunately, the same style in the hands of a manager with the power of job life and death creates unhealthy intimidation. "If the boss knows it all, why should I argue?" says the ordinary staff member. The staff member, however, may not realize that the boss is still very negotiable. The potential cost of immediately taking a strong, even intimidating position, however, may result in something a manager should want to avoid: shutting down any healthy opposition.

Managers need to learn not to take positions too early and to leave room for possible challenges that don't create excessive risk for the challenger. They should be more generous and let the argument run its course, even with the most timid of staff members. In the end, they might gain fresh insights that could lead to more productive results.

## LESSON #29

### Getting the Inside Story

Probably the most insensitive behavior of a manager is to discount people's feelings. No matter how minor a staff member's concern, complaint, or fear seems to be, the way that person feels about a situation is of major importance. Too often, managers are quick to discount those feelings, often with some dismissive remark such as, "I think you're making too much of this, George." George then cuts off the rest of his comments, which may be very important to the manager. He thinks to himself, *Why should I go on if the boss discounts whatever I say?*

If you want the story behind the story when there is one, you have to generously give time and attention to people as they are. Discounting others' feelings is a turnoff for most people. Here are a few turnoff examples:

1. A person complains to his manager that the big boss never says "Good morning" to him. The manager responds, "Oh, I'm sure he means to. He's just got important things on his mind."
2. A group of paralegals tells their lead attorney that the firm's managing partner passes them in the hall and never speaks, which indicates to them that he doesn't know who they are. Manager: "I'm sure you're wrong. He knows everyone in the firm," or, "He doesn't have to know you for you to get your work done."
3. In anger, a person, trying to get the shipping department on the phone, says to her boss, "Those shipping people are stupid and incompetent." Manager: "Now, you know, all of them can't be that way, can they?"
4. A supervisor tells the manager that he's afraid of missing his objectives because his group is decimated by illness and his best people have been promoted. Manager: "That simply gives you a greater challenge, doesn't it?"

Give people room to express their feelings. Don't patronize, deny, preach, or indirectly tell them to forget it. Instead, take time to empathize with your staff. More often than not, what you will discover is a concern behind the initial complaint that may have less than positive consequences for your business if it is not brought out and dealt with.

## LESSON #30

### Love Your Vendor as Yourself

Often vendors are the largest part of a project's cost. Certainly they can be the biggest factor for your productivity and cost improvements. The less vertically integrated businesses are, and the more parts and services that are purchased, the more paramount becomes the issue of dependable, quality-driven vendors. Even so, too many corporate people treat vendors as if they are less than human, replaceable parts, or rip-off artists who are not to be trusted. Here's an authentic memo from a CEO to his management consultant:

George:
   I really appreciate your squeezing a little time for me late in the day last week to let me use you as a sounding board in my thinking process on what to do about the department. That conversation was very useful to me in coming to my final conclusions.
   Jim and I had lunch together Tuesday afternoon, and after 2½ hours, Tom and I told him that he was the new head of

his department and the newest executive vice president of the company. The final announcement was made today.

Thanks to you for helping me get my head together. What would I do without you?

This kind of memo reflects class and stirs the vendor to new heights of commitment and performance.

This is why one should love one's vendor as oneself:

1. Corporate success often depends on vendors being conscientious, quality driven, and committed to the customer's and client's goals, both short- and long-term.
2. Vendors are people too!
3. Although not full-time employees, vendors often are, in effect, part-time employees, often for many years.

So you need to respect them as you would any colleague:

- Return their phone calls promptly.
- Answer their letters.
- Pay them promptly as agreed upon.
- Deal in a straightforward manner—no dangling! No lies! No games! No false promises!
- Tell and show them how their work affects the company's output.
- Tell them directly when they aren't meeting performance standards.

- Give them ready access to those controlling their work.

If you do these things, you have a right to expect that they will:

- Break their necks for you when needed
- Lose money sometimes or share the risk when it will help you
- Be straight with you—no games
- Promote good will for you in your marketplace

If you really want to get the biggest bang for your vendor buck, then "love your vendor as yourself."

## LESSON #31

### What Are Friends For?

What do you do when your boss tells you in confidence that he's firing your best friend? If you'd demonstrated a dislike for insider confidences in the past, he probably wouldn't have told you. But the die is cast, so consider these factors:

1. Does your boss know of your friendship? If so, why would he tell you and put you on the spot? Is he trying to gain your sympathy for his action, thus neutralizing you in the potential conflict? In other words, how honorable are his intentions and what does he expect from you?

2. How fair does your boss plan to be in the separation?
3. What advantage would it give your friend to know before being told by your boss?
4. What harm will it do the company or your boss if you secretly warn your friend?

After all this has been considered, then make your decision. All things being equal, and if the situation couldn't be avoided in the first place, many would risk telling their best friend.

Nothing is as important as the people in your life about whom you care and who care about you. They are lifetime lifelines. In the book of Genesis, Jacob, because he was hungry, sold his inheritance (the future) for a bowl of soup (the now). You can do the same when you accept confidences that hurt or destroy people for whom you really care.

# CHAPTER FOUR

\*

# Respect

WHEN YOU THINK of the disrespect you have experienced in the past, you may remember with some pain an intrusive parent who read your personal mail and nosed about your room to find out what you were up to. You may recall a teacher or coach who constantly interrupted you or who couldn't remember your name. But that was in childhood. Now you expect to be treated respectfully as a person. Whatever your education, status in life, appearance, or job function, you want to be shown esteem and to be treated with consideration and regard.

As a manager, it's important to treat others with respect. When you don't seek your staff's advice or their opinion on matters that affect their work—or even bother to say hello in the hall—you not only don't empower them, you enfeeble them. Any continuous pattern of behavior that is disrespectful may undermine their self-confidence and impair their performance, making your staff check with you constantly. Speaking behind the backs of your colleagues with disdain may create blocks to cooperation.

When a manager consistently behaves disrespectfully, he may drive off all but the sycophants or overly dependent employees (as is so often the case with overly self-impressed entrepreneurs). The only ones to survive will be those who absorb blows to their self-esteem in order to retain their income or position.

Not showing respect for others is usually a reflection of the lack of respect managers have for themselves, although some managers are just not aware of their impact on others. But without a doubt, the issue is important to sensitive and insensitive alike. I've never met an employee of a company who said, "I don't care if my manager respects me."

In the years ahead, more diversified business contacts will demand an increasing awareness of how various cultures show respect. You will have to learn how to show respect to your Japanese partner, your Native American employee, your Southeast Asian vendor, your Italian customer, and your German owner. If we don't even know how to show respect to American associates, what will we do to non-American associates?

In this chapter, the lessons point up the often unacknowledged slights and the intended as well as unintended putdowns all of us experience. The fundamental lesson is to understand that what conveys disrespect to others may not seem disrespectful to you. That doesn't mean something is wrong with them or with you. It simply means you have to respect those differences and manage sensitively in our global village.

## LESSON #32

### Stop Signs

There are married couples who can carry on long conversations in which they alternate in finishing each other's sentences. To some observers, this seems remarkable; to others, endearing. But such behavior is neither remarkable nor endearing when a supervisor finishes a staff member's sentences. Rude is a word that probably comes to most people's minds. Other words probably come to the staff member's, who feels that whatever he is thinking or trying to say has already been thought of or said by the boss.

But there is a more subtle, and probably worse, form of interruption. We have all observed this at some time, maybe even been active participants. This time it isn't words but actions that cut the speaker short: a cleared throat, a glance at a watch, a look into the hall, a sigh, even pausing without explanation to answer the phone.

A highly placed manager, the right hand of a CEO, was having a particular problem with his boss. When his boss was through listening to him in meetings, which could be in the middle of a thought or a sentence, the boss would raise his hand with the flat palm pointed toward him in a traffic cop gesture. Obviously, this greatly upset the manager, and he wished his boss would take him aside and talk to him privately if he was waxing too eloquently on unimportant points.

That traffic cop gesture communicated to the manager that the CEO thought he owned him, and that he would put up with anything in order to get his paycheck. To the manager's colleagues, who sometimes witnessed the hand signal, it communicated that the CEO did not hold him in high esteem, which undermined his effectiveness with his associates. There is also a touch of a poor parent—a parent who knows no other way to quiet a mouthy child—in the traffic cop gesture.

If you feel that any of your folks overtalk consistently, take them aside and be direct. You can't afford to publicly undermine their effectiveness. Nonverbal gestures of any kind are very powerful. A thumbs-up sign from someone you respect is a wonderful reward. Touching a person appropriately increases your impact by tenfold. Waving, giving an OK sign or big smile, and clapping your hands are all powerful and positive gestures. Used thoughtfully and carefully, positive gestures can speak volumes. Unfortunately, so can negative ones.

## LESSON #33

### The Executive "Editor"

A manager in an aerospace firm actually had to have thirty-two sign-offs from upper management for a decision. It wasn't just a matter of collecting all these signatures, however. Every one of the thirty-two had to edit something in the document—substitute a word, shift a sentence, change a pronoun, chop out material as redundant, suggest an expansion of the so-called redundant material. We're not talking about substance here, but style.

At another firm, the same type of editing occurred, except on a grander scale. Not only did the original writer have to deal with the various editing jobs of his superiors, he then had to send the document back for approval. The result was that the document would be re-edited, and often he found that a manager had changed his own correction back to what the writer had originally submitted! Finally, he stopped submitting what he considered his best work, since he knew it would never be appreciated.

All this can make a full-time job out of producing a document that is supposed to merely support the job. Such over-editing of letters, proposals, plans, and reports shows a lack of sensitivity to the other person's way of saying things.

If you find yourself wanting to edit a staff member's work because it really needs such attention, then you are misplacing that attention. You should coach, or assign someone to coach, the staff member on how to organize and clearly present ideas. Then ask to see an early draft of a document. That will allow you to make suggestions on what should be added or deleted and how it should be phrased. You should not do the work. That's your staff's job. Editors belong in only one field: publishing.

Eventually, with the right coaching, the staff member should be producing suitable documents. If there are phrasings that you would not use but that still get the points across clearly, let them alone. They represent the distinctive voice of that staff member. Allow it to sing. Over time, you'll learn to appreciate the tune.

## LESSON #34

### The Rainbow Workplace

This is an era of diversity. And for minorities to be heard, the majority may have to shut up—or be shut up—and learn. This doesn't mean you have to believe in establishing two or three official national languages. It does mean managers—especially white male managers—need greater sensitivity to majority language characteristics that contain codes of disrespect for minorities and women. In the past, minorities and women have tolerated, but inwardly winced at, such expressions as, "We have to scalp the competition," or, "We only want ballsy people here." Today such language is not to be tolerated.

You are certainly aware of the inappropriateness of certain words and phrases. These include the obvious—*broads, girls* when the women are over 16, *men* when *people* are intended, and the more subtle ones such as *BMW* for *B*lack *M*an *W*ishes.

For other words and phrases, however, there are no clear rules. To use them or not may depend on the circumstances, which means trouble because people have their own sensitivities. One guide managers can follow is simply to pay attention to what is reported in the news. For example, if most in a certain minority prefer to drop one term used to describe them in order to embrace another, then the new term is the one that should be employed by others who are not members of that minority.

No matter what your position, you must deal with people, and all people and their customs are worthy of respect.

## LESSON #35

### A Good Critique Is Not Always a Rave

Nearly everyone dislikes being criticized, and many people, are reluctant to offer criticism, especially to colleagues and certainly to their direct reports. Even a single inept criticism delivered offhandedly or with brutal honesty can have a devastating effect on a worker's morale and ability to perform well, as well as on his faith that you have his well-being in mind.

But criticism is necessary for a person to grow and develop. People need information every day as to how their performance stacks up against your expectations. The better this is done, the less important the annual performance review becomes.

When criticizing someone's behavior, then, it is important to bear two things in mind. First, the criticism should be constructive. Remarks such as "You don't even try," or, "Maybe you'll never learn," or, "Why don't you ever listen?" tend to be harsh to all of us because they are attacks that appear to provide the receiver no way out. They aren't giving guidance to do whatever should be done the next time.

Secondly, don't appear harsh. How harsh is harsh depends on the individual and his perception of your intent. Some people seem able to take anything. Others seem to have exceptionally thin skins. Defects such as continued poor judgment—leaving clients on hold forever, telling a customer to go somewhere else if they don't like the service, unnecessarily discounting costs—all violate the most common principles of common sense. But blasting the offending staff member seldom leads to more than making that person duck lower and own up less. It also creates negative and dysfunctional impressions of you in the minds of others.

Stick to criticisms that enable the other person to make some change. Provide fact-based information. Express emotion to convey the priority you place on new behaviors, but always take into account people's natural vulnerability to criticism, their need to save face, and your need to have them continue to work in open, collegial ways.

## LESSON #36

### The "Home" Office

The old expression, "Familiarity breeds contempt," certainly seems true in organizations. Unfortunately, this can even be true for managers who can too quickly treat their staff members with contempt because they see them so often or because they feel they "own" them.

When staff members enter your office, they are entering not just your office but your space—your house—and they should be treated as a host would treat a guest. In line with this assumption, you, the host, would:

1. Get up from your chair to greet staff members when they come in rather then simply ignoring them until you're ready to address them as some bosses do.
2. Make sure they're comfortably seated. Often employees feel ill at ease, uncertain whether they should sit on the couch, at the table, or across from your desk.
3. Speak in a tone similar to one you would use when greeting a guest in your home, not as if you are addressing a servant or a hired hand.
4. Walk them to the door when they leave. A wave of the hand in dismissal makes people feel as if they're beneath your respect.

Now, suppose the situation is reversed and you're the guest in the staff member's office. There are some common courtesies that we usually remember when we're in people's homes but often forget when we enter their offices.

1. Have you just come in from outside with wet or muddy shoes or rubbers? Could those footprints

on the carpet be yours? You wouldn't track dirt into a person's living room, would you?

2. Did you set your briefcase or, worse, coffee cup down in the middle of the final draft of a report the employee has worked on all month? Hold the cup or request a coaster.

3. Would you prop your feet up on the coffee table in the person's home? Is that any different from putting them on the employee's desk? Keep your feet on the floor—even when given permission to prop them up.

4. Have you rearranged the host's office furnishings for your convenience or comfort during the visit? If so, return them before you leave.

However the situation goes, if you act like a host or a guest, your staff members will undoubtedly respond in the same manner.

## LESSON #37

### Betrayed

After the board of a high-tech company decided to sell off one of its divisions, the vice president in charge of it was asked to head up a team that would handle the sale. For months, he led his division and worked hard to show it to best advantage to potential buyers. After many months with no real takers, the company, with his concurrence, spun off the division to be a free-standing company. The idea was to change the company's business mix, receive public money, and dump some debt on the new company.

Again, the vice president led the effort to keep up morale, reorganized the new division, and worked with the bankers and customers, with no guarantee from the selling company that he would be protected. He'd always considered himself a company man, and therefore assumed the best, that he would probably become the new chief executive officer.

On the day the spin-off was announced he discovered through the chairman's secretary that another vice president, who had not even been a part of the divestiture process, was to be named CEO of the new company. He was flabbergasted, both regarding the decision itself and the way he'd been left out of the decision-making process. The chairman had never counseled with him, never communicated with him or commiserated with him. His new boss asked him to remain on with the company as chief operating officer. Being loyal and recognizing that only with his operational experience and customer knowledge could the jobs of the people in his former organization be retained, he chose to remain.

The point is not whether the selling company's chairman had the right to act. What made the vice president bitter first of all was that he felt he deserved the new job of CEO of the spin-off company. But more important, he had known the chairman for twenty-seven years, and he hadn't received a courtesy call with an explanation of why the position was being given to another person.

This man will always be bitter and somewhat

angry because he felt betrayed, no matter what the intentions were of the selling company's chairman. Given his investment, his boss and friend of many years should have brought him in and taken the risk of an argument in order to share the reasons for the decision to select another candidate. That would at least have been the respectful thing to do.


## LESSON #38

### VIP Defined

Smart business people would say that any customer is a VIP. Once you begin embarrassing or treating any customer unresponsively, you're on the road to ruin, unless your marketplace has somehow avoided market forces.

One jewelry store gives you as much attention for a $10 pair of earrings as for a $25,000 necklace. They believe that if you're buying, you're a VIP.

In one airline VIP lounge, a gentleman and his wife had entered prior to their flight in a somewhat large crowd. He'd flashed his entry card as they walked in. In a few minutes, he was requested to return to the desk at the entrance. Here the attendant told him his was only a temporary card that he'd been issued to encourage him to try out the lounge. Now, however, she told him he couldn't stay because the date on the temporary card had expired.

He apologized but asked if he and his wife could

stay on this time. He was told, "Not unless you pay me for a permanent card."

The gentleman's face was getting red as he responded, "You mean to tell me that unless I pay your fee this moment you'll make my wife put her coffee back and force us to leave?" The attendant responded, "Yes."

Now he really began to yell about the lack of responsiveness to people that the attendant and the "damn airline" were wont to have. All of this at the top of his voice. Everyone in the lounge was hanging on every word as the attendant, now standing rigidly, pointed toward the door.

The man roared across the room, grabbed his startled wife by the arm, took their luggage, and with a few more epithets stormed out of the VIP lounge.

Of course, he may have been trying to slip one over. On the other hand, he may have sincerely missed the expiration date. But he hadn't asked for what he called "the damn card" that the airline had sent him, obviously considering him a VIP.

In any case, he should have been treated with respect. Everyone within earshot will long remember what happened to this couple, and some will take another airline whenever possible. Others may not sign up for the VIP lounge again.

Finally, one might wonder why her colleagues had made no move to help the now frightened and immobilized attendant out of the mess she and the airline had created.

Any customer is a VIP. Never embarrass customers so that they become tempted to embarrass you. That's risking a lot for a little.

## LESSON #39

### Strong Talk

The best use of profanity, if it is to be used at all, is to express an emphasis that only profanity can communicate, such as when you hit your finger or miss a one-foot putt in a high-stakes golf tournament. Too many managers, however, use profanity the same way they did in junior high school, some even sprinkling four letter words throughout tirades to their staffs.

Sometimes the target of the profane tirade is an individual. At other times, profanity is not directed at an individual, but rather at a situation that seems to elude all attempts at correction. Sometimes it is used for emphasis, which may not be necessary—especially when it contradicts a staff member's values. For example, the boss may say, "Goddammit, George, you had better get that article approved or it won't be just your ass but everyone else's in your department!" George's religious background may be such that the use of God's name in this context is not only unsavory but also frightening.

The point is, the curser has no right to violate other people's religion or any other sensibilities, especially if the curser is the boss and he uses this fact to excuse himself from the usual social restraints of speaking in any manner he wishes to the staff member.

In general, emphasis can be communicated without profanity. Profanity usually indicates at least a limited vocabulary and also, more often than any of us knows, betrays our anxiety and makes the other person feel put down. There should be a respect and an accommodation of others' value systems, especially those with less organizational power.

Using profanity only under circumstances where others can share the emotional emphasis it brings is acceptable, but never use profanity to prove you're tough, prove you're the boss, prove you're upset, frighten another person, intimidate another person, intentionally violate another person's values, or for shock value. It's just disrespectful.

## LESSON #40

### If Looks Could Kill

Ah, those knowing looks. They happen in meetings all the time. Sometimes the look says, "Aha, I told you so." Other times it's, "Well, what do you think of that?" or, "What bull that is. Don't you agree?" But perhaps the worst looks are those all-knowing and superior smiles exchanged while someone is talking.

Those looks are only the tip of an agenda, hidden, like an iceberg, and waiting to sink ideas or individuals. They can be aimed at a boss or someone deemed "out of it" or at a person who is resentfully seen as the boss's playmate or favorite. The looks can send signals of malice, contempt, or even fear. Whatever the emotions, they all show disrespect and discourage open participation by others, who may fear becoming objects of this silent conspiracy. These looks are disrespectful and rude. At the very least, they reflect insensitivity or naïveté on the part of the participants who, like adolescents in a classroom, don't think they are being observed.

The next time you are aware of exchanges of this kind at a meeting, take the people aside, especially if they are your peers or reports, and let them know their silent glances speak volumes better left unsaid. If that doesn't work, in the next meeting ask the people with the knowing looks what they think is wrong with what's being said. If they report directly to you, you can press them for an answer. If they are not your staff members, at least it will embarrass them sufficiently to get them to stop.

Don't let disrespect go unchallenged.

## LESSON #41

### When *Not* to Report to the Home Office

Company picnics, cocktail parties, or holiday get-togethers can be great occasions, giving colleagues a chance to relax with each other and to meet the others' spouses or close friends. But a boss, who holds power over people's jobs and thus their families' incomes, must be careful what he says at these functions. In particular, a boss must watch what he says to spouses—no matter how much they are recognized as supporting their mates' careers—either in praise or in criticism.

Sometimes the criticism is only implied: "Has John been drinking too much lately, Jane?" or, "Mary seems to have lost interest in her job. Is everything all right at home?" Later, John is bewildered when he learns of this criticism. Mary is upset that the boss is poking around in her private life.

Even praise becomes a double-edged sword: "Jane, I don't know what you're feeding Tom, but he sure has gotten more invested in his work. Whatever it is, you'd better give me some for the rest of the staff!" Later, Tom says to Jane, "I wonder what he meant by that? I didn't know I'd ever been slacking off."

Sometimes an implied criticism, or even praise, to a spouse when a marriage is in trouble can become new kerosene to be poured on the fires of difficulty at home. For example, "Your boss said he admires your total dedication to your work. Well, I could tell him that you certainly aren't that dedicated to me or the children."

A boss has both a formal power and an informal power, and the latter must be used sparingly and with discretion.

## LESSON #42

### The Intrusive Manager

You probably have either had personal experience with intrusive managers or have had stories related to you by those who have, so some of the characteristics are familiar. To list only a few:

1. Intrusive managers call you at any time (night, day, weekends) and expect you to drop what you're doing to meet their needs.
2. They read your mail before you get it. Sometimes they send it to others whom they think should see it before you see it! Sometimes they note on the letter how you should respond.
3. They interrupt your telephone conversations with an interrupt device provided by the phone company.
4. They demand that you stop your meeting and come to their office for an "important" (but unexplained) reason.
5. They consider your time and calendar totally available at their whim.
6. They have every call to you recorded by an operator for their later review.
7. They send you a memo demanding answers to complex questions that require you to stop everything else for as long as a day.
8. They give you a responsibility, then take it over themselves.
9. They have someone go through your personal papers to get something they need when you aren't in your office.
10. They go through your wastepaper basket after you leave each day.

Intrusive managers are people who lack respect for other human beings. No matter how charming they are or how attracted you are to them, keep in mind that their overt intrusion can only get worse. If

you've worked with one of these creatures, then you
know it can be hell. And you also know there's no
changing them. If you work for one now—or antici-
pate working for one—then get a written, personal
contract that allows the intrusive manager to commit only certain stated horrors and not others. And
good luck.

## LESSON #43

### "And There'll Be No Discussion"

It's probably happened to many of us at one time
or another. We're summoned to the boss's office to
hear the latest potentially controversial strategy or
tactics on a project. The boss lays it out—efficient-
ly, forcefully—then ends the monologue with the
phrase, "There'll be no discussion." This strikes you
as reminiscent of your dad laying down the law to
you in high school.

As one manager has pointed out, "It's a cardinal
sin not to allow discussion. There must always be
room for discussion. People need to be involved in
discussion that affects them. We should encourage
their participation, even though it may take time
and patience to do so."

Just as offensive is the boss who calls in a staff
member to bawl him out and does not allow that person to defend himself, explain, or offer any decent
excuse. Instead, the boss cuts short all discussion
by saying something like, "I'm sure it's true, and
nothing you can say will change my mind."

The result of not allowing discussion is to undermine confidence and cut off future help from staff
members. It's taking unfair advantage of your leverage over your staff. You don't have to agree with
what a staff member says or change your mind about
the decision, but you must listen courteously to the
expressed concerns, gripes, options, opposition, or
reasoning—assuming they are also expressed in a
courteous fashion.

You'd probably not be happy if you were treated
in this manner, so you should guard against using
your superior position in this way toward your staff.
Being bigger organizationally puts the burden of
being respectful first on you.

# CHAPTER FIVE

*

# Consideration

IN A GLOBALLY competitive environment, pressures for quality, more personal accountability, faster development cycles, and restructuring of companies are extreme. As the pressures mount, so does dysfunctional stress. To counter this stress, managers need to share with their staffs the joys, sorrows, failures, successes, and their own appreciation for work well done. Stress is a large factor in the workplace and will increase in importance. The manager who is concerned for others as individuals and does not simply view them as interchangeable parts can greatly reduce that stress and make the workplace a source of support for the times when personal lives seem devoid of caring and are in great confusion.

Such confusion begins early in many people's lives: Home buying, divorce, being a single parent, sickness, addiction, living instability. As the work force gets older, crises such as disease, death, and personal tragedies beset us. The job, the company, and one's supervisor may be all that keep a person together. The workplace becomes an emotional anchor, a place to go where one can achieve, feel some ownership of one's destiny, and rebuild some self-esteem.

A company president, who was formerly bottom-line-only, came to a new conclusion: "Love is as important in the workplace as the bottom line." Caring for each other builds cohesion, teamwork, and the motivation to perform at unexpectedly high levels. Since people spend more time in the workplace than anywhere else, why not make it a place to be and to become, a place of pride. "LOVE means *l*ots *o*f *v*aluable *e*mployees."

In Japan, supervisors in many companies are expected to attend the funerals of their staff's family members—often to be the chief speaker—as well as to attend weddings and other significant personal events. But in the United States, many companies discourage managers from knowing their people personally. These companies seem to want work and personal life completely separated. Sometimes the reason given is that it's hard to fire people when you get too close to their lives. So it's not easy being a manager, but people go with the territory, don't they?

Such divisions between management and workers weren't present in the entrepreneurial companies in the early 1900s. At that time, company presidents knew their employees well enough to know who would be in the tank on Monday morning and would need to be bailed out. People who had performed well might request and be granted advanced salaries in troubled times. While that period may have been too paternalistic, we have swung too far the other way.

The manager can create a healthy personal milieu without sacrificing performance. In fact, showing consideration for people reduces stress and creates an environment where the single mother, the older employee, the ambitious night school immigrant, the white kid interning in the engineering department, or the black kid helping his folks, can, with your help, perform beyond your expectations and theirs.

Here, then, are some lessons that show how being considerate is not only kind, but also rewarding both personally and professionally.

## LESSON #44

### Crossed Wires

Many people find electronic (E-mail) or voice mail excellent ways to leave messages for someone at times when they can't be reached any other way. It's wonderful when you need no immediate response. It's comforting not to have to worry whether a secretary delivered your message in the content and the tone you wanted. It's great when you can call the United States from Europe at a reasonable time and leave a voice message that can be heard by the recipient at a reasonable hour in America. But there are times when managers take unfair advantage of these new forms of communication.

Don't get to the office at 5:00 A.M. and leave twenty-five messages of instruction for each of your direct reports. One manager who does this causes quiet resentment because each day his staff spends all their time simply carrying out his orders for the day.

Don't just ramble and dump lots of words into the box without thinking of the time of the poor people at the other end. They have to listen, especially if you're the boss. Those messages should be crisp, clear, and to the point. Think and outline before you talk.

Don't have your secretary's voice mail answer your calls. Callers still have no idea if their messages will get through, which defeats one of the original purposes of using this medium.

Avoid using one-way electronic media in any form to simply slam-dunk a decision that brooks no dispute. That's cowardly.

Don't say or put nasty, confrontative things on the computer E-mail that you don't feel able to say to the person face-to-face.

In other words, remember that electronic communication devices do not remove all the constraints that normal face-to-face communications demand. Such technology will continue to be developed, but no matter what the advances, normal rules of consideration will always apply.


## LESSON #45

### Pillow Talk

In these days of enlightened perspective, it's considered noble to declare, "I don't take my troubles home. I leave them at the office." The problem with this practice is that it excludes a spouse from over half of an individual's waking hours.

With one out of every three marriages ending in divorce in the United States, maybe we'd better try something new. We all have our ups and downs at work. To hide them from that very important person in your life can cause other problems. Tell your spouse how you are getting along with others, what ideas you came up with that day, who you like or dislike and why, who's causing you trouble—even what's worrying you most!

True, your spouse may develop a bias toward people you're having trouble with. But, so what? Your spouse is on your team and *should* be biased. If spouses can resist being biased, they sometimes make the best coaches. The person you married knows your strengths and weaknesses, so why not use that knowledge to your advantage.

Of course, you need to gauge how close-mouthed your spouse is or how well he or she can handle situations that involve people who've caused you trouble. On the whole, however, it's better to risk telling a spouse your concerns, anxieties, fears, and ambitions than not to. Your spouse has a stake in you that is greater than any corporation!

If you are not married, the same advice holds true for whoever takes up space, if not in your home, then in your heart. It could be a lover, a family member, or a close friend. Everyone could benefit from personal support and an out-of-the-office perspective, if only to act as a sounding board. Show consideration

for them. Include them in issues you spend a full
third of your life addressing.

## LESSON #46

### The Medium Is *Not* the Message

There's an old story about a railroad passenger
who found a dead cockroach on his bunk in the train.
He wrote the president of the railroad complaining
about the incident. Some time later he received a very
nice letter, presumably from the president, apologizing for the inconvenience caused by finding a cockroach. Also accidentally included was the traveler's
original letter. It had a handwritten note in one
corner that read, "Send him the cockroach letter."

No one likes "cockroach letters." We all receive
them, and we all know they are form letters. Form
letters are precisely that: form, without substance.
They do not communicate that someone has heard
you or cares about your problem. Any communication is all about substance, about having heard what
the sender has to say, seriously considering it, and
then acknowledging the situation.

Form can help that communication, and not paying attention to form signals that you think little
of your substance. But form can also hinder, and
it should not itself be the message. When it is, the
message we're getting is, "I don't have time for you,
and you aren't important enough for me to worry
about."

When you think about the form letters you've

received, you may agree that it's better not to have received any answer than what was insensitively mailed off to you. When you have to respond to any complaint in writing, make it personal. No cockroach letters, please.

## LESSON #47

### "And While You're at It, Tell Him to Forget It!"

A vice president and general manager was reviewing a personal travel request of the director of engineering. The request was obviously ill-timed and showed the director's insensitivity to the division's financial needs. In response to the request, the general manager called his secretary in, handed her the request, and said to her in an angry voice, "You tell him there's absolutely no way he can leave during that time period, and it's stupid of him to ask. Tell him to forget it!"

Another general manager, upset because assembly of a new chip board was in danger of missing a delivery date, called his director of production. When the director's secretary answered and said her boss was not in the office, the general manager launched into a diatribe about the director's lack of commitment to the project and insisted that the secretary tell the director—"word for word"—what the general manager had said.

Now, while good secretaries will obviously translate for irate bosses, managers shouldn't be dependent on such secretarial skills to keep them from looking like high-handed SOBs.

In the first instance, the general manager owed the director an explanation for the rejection of the travel request. If the director was really so insensitive to the effect of his actions, this was an opportunity for the general manager to teach him. If the travel request seemed out of character, perhaps there was more than met the eye in that request. In the second situation, that general manager should have left a message for the production head to contact him rather than dumping on his secretary. Perhaps the reason for the director's absence from his office was because he was on the plant floor trying to meet a tight deadline.

In both cases, if the general managers were so upset, they should have communicated directly, on the phone or face-to-face, so that their reports would be clear about the message. It would also relieve the secretaries from being potential punching bags for their bosses. In that way, consideration can be shown to all.

## LESSON #48

### "Isn't It a Shame?"

When managers suddenly find themselves fired, the usual first reaction among colleagues, especially if they care for the individual even a little, is to say, "Isn't it a shame?" But why attach shame to being fired? In some situations, it may actually be the best thing that could happen.

Too often, though, that's where the sympathy stops: commiserating with colleagues rather than sympathizing with the fired person. Personally reaching out to such an individual is one of the most gracious things you can do.

Write and tell your former colleague or boss the specific things you'll miss when you're no longer working together. Call the person at home, if necessary, and share your disappointment and support, even if you've never called there before. Call or write again after a month if your former colleague is still unemployed.

People are always in pain when they're fired, and they may feel quite alone and vulnerable. A simple human gesture, even from people they don't know well, can mean a great deal at this time of separation.

The same is true for other significant experiences you hear about, such as when people lose family members, have car accidents, or have operations. Reach out! They'll love it. "I don't know what to say," you may say. Quit worrying about yourself. Just tell them or write them what's in your heart.

One tough-minded executive had a serious car accident in which his face was badly damaged. A consultant who had worked with him only slightly wrote him a note wishing him well and telling him of a similar accident he'd been in years before. Over a year later, the executive reached across the table to shake the consultant's hand and thank him profusely for having taken the time to write.

Don't tiptoe around other people's pain. Reach out and address it.

## LESSON #49

### Advice That Leads to Consent

Part of a manager's job is to give instruction or advice, sometimes solicited, sometimes not. Regardless, it should never be gratuitous. Here are two approaches to consider.

First, if your instructions are to put pressure on staff to make changes they don't want to make, be courteous enough to carefully and sympathetically state the staff members' case so that they know you understand their feelings. Most people think that if you don't agree with them, you couldn't possibly have understood. It's important to acknowledge the problems your instructions may cause your staff, letting them know that you have fully considered their thoughts and are concerned about them personally. Now, even though they may still not like the change, they will more than likely comply cooperatively, if not enthusiastically. You have allowed them to save face.

The other approach is used when managers want to give advice and influence to subordinates in some way without giving them a directive. The best approach is simply to say to the staff member, "Kathy, I'd like to make a couple of suggestions for you to consider." Then wait for an invitation to continue.

This approach gives the other person due respect. Kathy may now say, "Of course, I'd like to hear."

Even if she's already made up her mind and isn't enthusiastic, she'll now give your thoughts some consideration. Had you simply dumped your advice gratuitously, it would either have run off like water from a duck's back, causing her to stiffen her resolve to do it her own way, or it would have made her overly dependent on your way of doing things. If she discourteously said, "No, I really don't want to hear your opinion!" you can still give the order, if necessary.

## LESSON #50

### "But It Can't Go Any Further Than This"

A staff member approaches you. "I need to tell you about Tom," he says softly. "It isn't particularly complimentary, and I sure wouldn't want to be quoted. Okay?"

Well, that's certainly seductive. You *do* want to know what Tom has said or done. Your staff member may think you're in competition with Tom and sense your vulnerability to criticism, or he may not like Tom, so he presents Tom to you in the worst light, first exacting a promise of secrecy from you.

There are confidences, and then there are confidences. Some are personal issues your staff talks over with you, using you as a sounding board. They may need you to be their chaplain at the moment, and it's okay to fill that role occasionally. Then there are the confidences when you are strategizing with others to change "unfair" policies of the firm or where others involve you unwittingly in enabling a disease, such as when you cover up for the on-the-job alcoholic forays of another staff member.

Some confidences are appropriate, but beware of being drawn in by an invitation to insider confidence that results in a collusion from which you feel honor bound not to escape.

People who are always saying, "I'd like to tell you something, but it obviously can't go farther" are working their own agendas, which never need encouragement; otherwise you'll have insider confidences on top of insider confidences, and you'll lose track of your real loyalties. If you allow yourself to be compromised so that someone gets hurt because you took an inappropriate confidence, you're not showing consideration for others.

## LESSON #51

### Tell Me Where I Stand

One woman manager complained that she had to go to a course on leadership to discover how highly her boss regarded her.

As a part of the course, she sent a questionnaire to her boss, her peers, and her staff members. The data she received back told her volumes about her boss's appreciation for her contribution. Never had he taken the time before to tell her where she stood. Never had she had the courage to ask.

People need to know where they stand. Where do they need to improve? Where are they satisfactory? When do they excel? This woman and her boss have developed an entirely new relationship as a result of the fresh data from the questionnaire. Her enthusiasm exceeds all bounds. His is equally positive regarding her performance. And now he's learned to tell her so she doesn't have to guess. He's found the value of praise.

Knowing where you stand doesn't mean bad news. Asking your boss, who may be quite reluctant, can help you get the data you need.

## LESSON #52

### Boss's Interruptus

Some bosses have no appreciation for the time or activity of staff members. One, for example, will walk up to two staff members who are chatting in the hall and simply break in without a by-your-leave to address one or both with what's on his mind. Whatever he wants takes precedence over the interaction he observed going on between the two. In fact, it may appear that he did this without realizing the consternation his interruption caused.

Another manager would do the same in a staff meeting. If a member was in the middle of a sentence and he wanted to move the group on, he'd simply break in and start the next subject, leaving the speaker in mid-sentence with his mouth open.

Still another manager would stick his head into

a staff member's office, breaking into any meeting going on, to say what he had to say at the moment he wanted to say it.

In some ways, the worst breach of etiquette is when the boss orders the staff member who is in the middle of his staff meeting to leave his meeting and come to the boss's office for some mysterious purpose.

In every case, there is no regard expressed for the other person's time or the priority of his activity. Be careful to avoid Boss's Interruptus. You don't own your staff members. Treat them as you would treat highly regarded friends. Remember, interrupting them without apology or clear cause sends ripples of incredulity through the organization about how much of a boor you really are. If you are insensitive to the impact of your interruptions on your staff members, you soon may have no staff members to interrupt.

A good rule is to never interrupt your staff in a way you wouldn't interrupt your own boss. For most, if not all, that will cure Boss's Interruptus.

## LESSON #53

### Not Invented Here

It's hard to find a company that isn't international, with global sales and global governance, or in complex alignments with companies outside the United States. As a result of this, managers often must relate to bosses who are foreign nationals, subordinates whose national loyalties lie other than with their own, or peers who are from a multitude of races, national identities, and industries.

When dealing with people from foreign organizations, it's wise to remember that all nationalities and races tend to be chauvinistic, and consider their way the right way. When such affinities are taken to their extreme and clash in the global marketplace, the results may be economic wars that can poison international relations or even become hot wars.

While one cannot know all there is to know about others, a new sensitivity is called for. We need to actively discover what are the breaking points in interpersonal and interorganizational relationships, and then avoid them like the plague.

What constitutes a serious breach of courtesy with a Japanese? What business assumptions most distress a Swede? What causes a Nairobi top talent to leave your employment? What social gaffe would cause a Bulgarian to disapprove your plant opening? In other words, what are the breaking points? Study them. Then decide if doing business globally will be successful if indeed you often find you cause the breaking of deals and aren't willing to change. It's better not to do business at all than to have to recover from a financial disaster.

Sensitivity, openness, self-examination, flexibility, interest in others' social and business ways, interest in their language, and looking to protect their interests as well as your own may get you over the hump of not-invented-here that all races and nationalities and companies tend to develop to protect their self-image and identity. And also beware of understanding the other culture or people "too deeply," which is called "going native," for one culture may end up being absorbed by the other. Those are the risks, but the benefit of global alliances far outweighs the risks of losing one's cultural or business identity.

## LESSON #54

### Bad Connections

We have an odd relationship with telephones. They are such impersonal, mechanical objects, yet we often assume that the medium not only creates instant access, but also allows us to act in ways that we would not if we were meeting someone in person. Some examples:

1. You call someone on your staff and launch into what you would like her to do. Your staff member, if she's on the job, is either up to her eyeballs in a project, reviewing a key contract with another staff member, or about to return a client's call.
2. As a busy manager, you sometimes have your secretary call and get someone on the line for you. You keep them on hold until you finish "just one last thing." Meanwhile, the person called is not doing much of anything, except perhaps thinking dark thoughts about you.
3. You call and get another manager's secretary. You don't bother asking how the secretary is

doing, even though if you met in person you would shake hands and exchange a few polite words. You wonder later, after a few calls, why it's getting more difficult to be put through to that manager.

4. You're in a meeting with a staff member and keep interrupting the conversation to answer your phone.

5. You're in your office and available to take calls, when you hear your secretary query a caller with, "May I ask who's calling?" implying that she or you will decide if the caller is important enough to talk to.

6. Your secretary is juggling two callers simultaneously when a third call rings in. She quickly answers the third line with, "Can you hold please?" and, without waiting for a response, returns to her previous conversation. In the several minutes it takes her to complete the first two calls, the third caller tires of waiting and hangs up. It's two days before you discover that you've missed a conversation with your most important customer who was calling from China.

Some suggested solutions:

Example #1. Until you get a viewphone that allows you to see if people you call are busy, ask if they have the time to deal with your needs.

Example #2. You called them and should be immediately available.

Example #3.  Orally "shake hands" and ask how the
person is.

Example #4.  Calls can wait, unless you've clearly
indicated to your guest why it's necessary to talk to the production department, which is on a tight deadline, or
with that potential account you've been
hoping to land.

Example #5.  There are people that you may not
want to talk to when you're in, and your
secretary should then be instructed. If
you want people put through to you,
then have your secretary ask, "May I
say who's calling?"

Example #6.  A few seconds of additional conversation to find out who is calling and where
they are calling from, even though it's
inconvenient, can save embarrassment, or worse.

Telephones may give us instant access, but they
don't give us permission to behave like instant
asses.

## LESSON #55

### Coming to Attention

One of the top four officers of a large U.S.–based
international corporation recently described a rather
humorous, but devastating, scene. He and the other
three officers had requested a presentation from

two European marketing folks. They came on the appointed morning and began to make their presentation.

While the presentation took place, the president went through his mail. As if taking their cue from their CEO, the other two officers began to go through their mail. The presenters droned on as if nothing was happening.

Sometimes organizations develop norms that support such bad manners and lack of consideration. One simply expects to be treated in shabby ways and, in turn, treats others shabbily without intending to.

In a people-oriented company, however, listeners pay attention to presentations—even dull ones. They ask questions, request elaboration, and offer encouragement, which can actually turn a poor presentation into a fairly good one. If a presenter, no matter how dull, isn't supported, everyone at that meeting is spending the corporation's money in foolish ways.

# CHAPTER SIX

## *

# Gratefulness

SO MANY PEOPLE believe they are "entitled." They are entitled to an education, three meals a day, a great house, summer and winter vacations, an exceptional salary, an interesting job, a terrific spouse, and children who are above average. The word that most misses the point is "entitled." We're entitled to almost nothing in this world, not even an easy birth.

What we call entitlements are really gifts from someone else—our God, our parents, our loved ones, our country, our company. Opportunities sometimes are the work of random chance. We were at the right place at the right time with the right stuff. But there are always people who are touting us, giving to us, caring for us, and sometimes bleeding for us. Truly, we aren't entitled. We are being gifted.

People who are grateful are grateful about everything. They may not have always had a pleasant life, but they find the parts that are good and are grateful. They essentially believe that although having talents, they were given breaks. They are truly grateful that their boss sees in them the skills, knowledge, and ability to promote them, emphasizing the boss's keen perception, not their rights and abilities. When their company springs for a party, or a customer writes a nice letter about them, or their colleagues break their necks to help them when they become seriously ill, they are grateful. They live in the mode of being grateful for what everyone does for them because they don't figure it was their due. They thank everyone who makes life easier. They appreciate the little things and they take no one and no pleasure for granted. Because they don't believe they have entitlements, they aren't embittered or devastated that things don't always go their way. They don't ask why bad things happen to good people. It never occurred to them that they were so good that it entitled them to only good things.

Unless these people are completely naive and not in touch with their own and others' pain, they are incredibly easy to work with. Their attitude is rarely sour and they truly see opportunities where the entitled see problems and despair.

As a manager, if you believe that anything good is strictly a gift, you approach working with others with an open heart and hand. You give compliments easily and show real appreciation that people do their jobs, even though they're being paid to do them.

Being grateful, though, doesn't mean not having high standards. High standards met by one's staff are something to be grateful for. Most people respond well to high standards and, when the boss shows true appreciation, will often try to exceed them.

This chapter can only be grasped by those willing to assume that we should expect nothing, but rather be eternally grateful for what we get. It is about living and loving with a childlike appreciation for whatever others do for you—and a plea to let them know how much their gifts mean to you.

Here, then, are lessons on gratefulness that often address areas where we might think we were entitled to what happened or what we got.

## LESSON #56

### Any Volunteers?

Some people think there are two kinds of workers, volunteers and those who get paid. Not true! There are only volunteers, some who get paid, and some who do not.

In every high-achieving organization, people are basically volunteers. If staff members don't really want to work but just collect a paycheck, they can do it (although it's becoming increasingly difficult to pull it off). They can daydream, talk with others about personal issues, gripe about management, read novels, take long lunch hours, dawdle, take sick days when they aren't sick—in short, produce just enough to get by.

The point is simple. If you treat people as

if they're lucky you've let them work in your organization or as if their reward for an outstanding job is that they get to keep their job, you soon find that you get minimum effort from them. In fact, in such an environment, one's peers will not even allow others to achieve above the minimum. Asking for stretch objectives will be received with yawns. Nothing extra is offered. Resistance is strong toward requests to work overtime. Favors can never be asked. People will move slower when you aren't watching them. So, you say, "I'll fire the ungrateful slobs!" Fine; but first you have to catch them, which is a full-time job.

What makes people "volunteer"? Why is it that some computer programmers produce thirty times more than others? Why is it that some people on NASA projects work seventy or more intense hours a week without being asked or paid extra for it? The truth is that whether people are employees or volunteers, they do what really needs to be done only voluntarily. Giving the extra smile to the customer, going the second mile to please you, being average but doing above-average work, being committed or getting a job done because of the company's reputation—are all driven by emotion, or some say passion, for which there is no monetary payment. People "volunteer" because the company or their colleagues expect their best and give them the best. And in particular, when you are enthusiastic and behave in the ways you want them to behave, you set the tone of voluntarism so necessary to a high-performing organization.

## LESSON #57

### Giving Thanks

It's always curious how people assume that what they have learned about certain courtesies doesn't apply in the workplace. There was an executive who spent a great deal of time shopping with his wife to select beautiful silver pitchers to send to all of his direct reports and their spouses as Christmas gifts. Of the eight families who received the gift, only two thanked him, and then only orally and weeks later.

For Aunt Matilda, who sent us that gaudy tie with Santas all over it, we learned a handwritten note of appreciation was in order—and sent within the week. A boss (or boss and spouse) deserve at least that consideration. Also, your boss should be thanked personally at your first opportunity when your paths cross in the workplace. It doesn't make any difference whether the company paid for the gift or the boss did. Your boss went to a great deal of trouble thinking of you. That's the real gift.

Sometimes the gift can be a clock with the company logo, an unexpected ride on the company airplane, company-owned tickets to your favorite concert group or sports event. Even if bosses don't pay out of their pockets, they did think of you and your needs, and they deserve to be thanked.

Sending a boss a gift in return is not at all expected, but considering that your boss is, in a certain sense, your customer, a simple thank-you note when your superior goes to the trouble of doing something for you is classy and reflects a life of gratefulness.

## LESSON #58

### Acknowledging the Right Stuff

Some time ago, a group vice president of a grocery company was surprised, bewildered, and hurt that, although he had fought to promote four vice presidents to divisional general managers, not one of them had conveyed appreciation for the opportunity or for his political maneuvering to get the promotions for them.

We all know that, in general, for promotions up to the director level the questions most asked by those promoting are, Is this person competent? Do they have the technical knowledge, experience, know-how, and the people skills to fill the open position? At the vice president level, the questions become more complicated. Competence, knowledge, experience, and people skills have generally been proven. Now the questions are, Have they got the judgment and maturity to make the broad decisions they will have to make? Have they been burned enough, failed and recovered so that confidence is built on a firm foundation? Are they my kind of person? Are they team players?

You'd think the recipient of such a promotion would recognize that promotion at this level is always more than a question of competence or of being deserving. If you have a desire to move up in responsibility, understand that each stage has different requirements. It's a big move from individual contributor to supervisor. It's another leap from manager to director of a function. It's even a greater leap to become an officer. While all promotions are based upon your abilities, hardly anyone has been so immaculately conceived as to not need a sponsor for each new leap forward.

Anyone who is promoted and thinks they deserve that promotion doesn't understand the real world. If someone intercedes for you, you may just be at the right place at the right time with the right philosophy and the right friends. Better to take those who are responsible aside and say, "I really appreciate your efforts on my behalf and hope I can demonstrate that you selected the right person." Better yet, also put it in writing.

## LESSON #59

### Praise Up!

There's risk in telling your boss he made a great speech, wrote a good report, or handled a client with great skill. First of all, he may think you are insincere, simply seeking an inside track with him. Perhaps, even worse, your colleagues may see your actions in the same light, whispering behind your back or treating you with disdain.

Your boss may also consider what you say as unnecessary because he thinks he knows how good he is already. Or perhaps he's been brought up to believe that "real men" don't compliment each other. So there is risk, but you should take the risk.

Bosses as human beings need praise from people they respect, including the people who report to them. In order to prevent your praise from being perceived as insincere, be specific. "Your analysis of the trends in our business hasn't appeared in any literature I've seen." "You really made me feel good about myself even though the criticism you gave me was on target." "I liked the way you handled the customer during your presentation, firm but respectful."

Because bosses tend to receive little praise, many top managers have learned not to care whether people like what they do or not. They become inured to praise or criticism.

Unfortunately, few of us think to compliment our supervisors for a job well done. This lack of deserving praise may in fact derive from the way we took our parents for granted. After all, they are our parents, why should they need praise? Maybe if they go back to college at fifty-five and graduate in two years. But should you really praise them for raising a successful family?

Yes, just as you should praise your boss for running a successful department or division. And yes, there is that risk, but take it. Praise up!

## LESSON #60

### Giving Extra Credit

At the end of a recent meeting of the top management of an 8,000-person division, the divisional vice president sincerely thanked the group vice president for taking time to come to the meeting and present his concerns from a group and corporate perspective. In addition, he publicly thanked the employee who had performed the nitty-gritty tasks of arranging ground transportation, rooms, flights, luggage handling, meeting facilities, and other necessities.

Obviously, the group vice president had a large stake in the division's performance. His presence at the meeting was self-serving. So why thank him? The divisional vice president recognized that the group vice president didn't have to treat this particular meeting as a priority.

Obviously, the individual who was caring for the meeting needs was getting paid. Why thank him? Because he had been particularly solicitous and obviously desired the event to be as positive as he could make it for everyone in attendance.

The divisional vice president made no caste distinction when it came to giving thanks. He knew that whether a person is a group vice president or a meeting planner, their willingness to go the extra mile is something that cannot be bought. His gestures of appreciation were sincere and impressive.

Staff members participating in tasks that are not

necessarily part of their regular assignments should also receive a thank-you. Volunteering for overtime when needed, getting the job done by working on weekends, serving on the Community Chest committee, representing the company on the local public television fund-raising campaign, or even filling out an employee attitude survey all deserve more than the usual paycheck.

As we have all experienced, there is no substitute for a thank-you for a job well done—in person, by handwritten note, on a report, or via the telephone. Whenever possible, do it in public. But don't do it gratuitously or effusively when it isn't deserved. Everyone sees through that.

## LESSON #61

### Cheerleading

One person's fascination can be another's boredom, especially in meetings. Someone keeps leaving the room to take phone calls. One reads his mail. Another talks privately to a neighbor. Yet another pushes the presenters to move along, thus rushing the presentations. We all get bored in meetings where our interests, concerns, or priorities aren't being dealt with. The real question is how to handle boredom when, for example, you are listening to your staff present their operational plans that you've already read in detail. If you think such a meeting—and your presence—are necessary, then you should be attentive. Asking questions that allow your staff members to shine and leading the applause after each presentation will not only keep you alert, but also show that you truly care about the presenters.

Your staff members are constantly looking to you for signs of approval, however small. Your actions cause reactions in almost everyone in your organization. They take their lead from you. Insensitive behavior, even more than words, ripples down the halls of an organization. "He did what?" "He wouldn't have done that!"

In your position of authority you want to be chief cheerleader. The crowd always has its third eye on your responses.

## LESSON #62

### What! No Parties?

A large *Fortune* 500 company decided to sell the defense segment of their portfolio, partly due to their projection that it would be unprofitable in a post–Cold War world, and partly because more and more of the public considered it a "dirty" business. But no one wanted it. So they spun it off, going public, while loading the new company with lots of debt. The company was financially strapped; it had too many people, too few orders, and extensive wasteful systems.

Over the years the company had paid for Christmas parties, birthday parties, celebrations of newly won or completed programs. It had sent strong technical contributors on boat trips and top sales people on European vacations. Everyone in the company had gotten used to a certain way of living.

In the new environment, however, management faced the real possibility that the company might not make it. To increase the chances for survival, they had to lay off scores of people, reorganize tightly, cut all the frills, and create more efficient systems. Above all, they had to have people understand there was a new situation. It would not be business as usual. This is similar to what any family has to do in tough times, but getting the attention of a family of four is a lot easier than getting the attention of 10,000 employees.

While there was much disruption, fear of failure, and anxiety over possible job loss among employees, the biggest emotional issue was management's decision to discontinue paying for parties. People had felt entitled and now felt cheated. They thought that the company owed them these parties, even though their colleagues were being laid off.

When tough times come to your company, it's important that you keep your perspective. Having a good job is paramount and a great gift. All else are lesser gifts, enriching but undeserved. Don't complain in hard times when the parties have to go. Be grateful for the opportunity to create a situation where they can once again be instituted.

## LESSON #63

### Loyalty

It used to be that many public schools taught key values in the fourth grade. These included loyalty, bravery, truthfulness, and honesty. These qualities have become associated with naïveté or provoke cynical sneers. This is unfortunate, because a great society and great companies are built on strong values, not just market share, computer-aided design processes, or sophisticated manufacturing techniques. To mock and deride values can truly undermine a company's fabric. In no way is this more true than in the case of loyalty.

Loyalty is a gift, a grateful response to those who've provided for and cared for you through thick and thin. It's what holds marriages, friendships, and business partnerships together during difficult times. It's what causes management to work hard to avoid layoffs or even to retain people beyond their time of productivity. It's behind the ready acceptance of employees to take cuts in pay and benefits in tough times. Loyalty is like what's in the bank with each other, voluntarily deposited.

The only way to get loyalty is to give it. When you are promoted, do not forget those who served you well. Don't just go to your good-bye party and disappear. These were your people. They were and are loyal. Don't forget their needs just because yours have been fulfilled.

A grateful person also offers the gift of loyalty to his boss, even before it's deserved. Some bosses aren't aware of the value of loyalty, so they won't appreciate the gift. Others may be awakened to it. Some may even try to exploit it. But offering it is important to a person who lives in a grateful manner.

Being loyal to management may at times conflict

with ethical choices they force on you. Then you
have to decide what's right for you. But, in general,
loyalty can win friends. It is:

1. Looking out for those who look out for you.
2. Not joining the opposition for personal gain.
3. Telling your boss when you know he's wrong or
   when what he is doing will get him in trouble
   even when he doesn't like it.
4. Not asking people who work for you to do anything that would jeopardize their career.
5. Finding ways to advance your people for their
   good and the company's good even when it may
   not be to your good.
6. Not writing off your people or your boss when
   they are going through personal crises that tem-
   porarily impair their productivity or sensitivity.
7. Never badmouthing your boss on any issue behind
   his back.
8. Taking responsibility for decisions of your boss
   and peers even when you don't agree with those
   decisions.

   That's loyalty!


## LESSON #64

### Where the Acorns Come From

One thing that's easy to do is to forget, like the pig
who never looks up, where the acorns come from.
Over the years there are people who go out of

their way to help you. One may voluntarily tell you of a better job that you might apply for. Another recommends you to another division, resulting in higher pay and opportunity. Still another may refer a customer to you, vouching for your integrity and ability.

For professionals, there's that moment when they are tapped by a professional society they wish to belong to. Someone, some specific person or persons, took the time to place their name in nomination.

Is there a nicer tribute than for a supervisor's employees, unknown to her, to nominate her for the company's annual Top People Manager Award?

How about the friend who visits with your adult child to help him find his way professionally or to get a job? Aren't those people special? Most of us generally appreciate these acts of kindness.

There are even less personal acorns that come into our lives, such as when an editor we don't know takes a liking to our writing. Or someone comes across a report we did and likes it well enough to independently send it to the company president.

While these incidents aren't as personal, remember, they were initiated by real people who admired something and helped you get ahead. They should be appreciated, where appropriate, through notes or through flowers or some other appropriate gift when they receive honors, promotions, or even setbacks. They should also, where reasonable, be given the edge by you when you have the power to help them.

People who truly act spontaneously on your behalf seldom feel you are obligated. That's what makes it

a joy to remember them, the rest of your life. Keep
a list! Call them ten years, twenty years later and
say thank you. It's fun and reminds you where the
acorns came from.

## LESSON #65

### Giving Back

Some managers' lives are totally absorbed in their
company's activities or in the pursuit of their own
pleasure or profit. They may take the children to
school activities, but that's because they're their
children. They may speak to a child's class on Career
Day, but again, it's because their child is in the class.
In other words, all activities are focused on them and
their family.

Being grateful means being focused on others as
well as yourself. Those others are the ones who've
provided an educational system, a reasonably order-
ly society, and a means by which you can optimize
your talents if you have the drive and the opportunities develop.

What does all this mean? It means giving back.
It means being involved in your church, your syna-
gogue, or your mosque. It means serving on community boards or those of nonprofit agencies, of participating in the Special Olympics or the United Way.
It means being involved in improving government
through voting drives or political fund-raisers or
even running for office. It may mean simply being
a volunteer at the polls on election day.

Giving back means giving money and time to your old school, to the education system, to minority needs, and to welfare causes.

In other words, being grateful means giving gladly and broadly in appreciation for what has been given to you from those who've gone before, even when there is no direct benefit to you, your family, or your company. It's a way of life that builds a society, and for those who want their own needs met, it's bread upon the water that, indirectly, will be returned tenfold.

# CHAPTER SEVEN

## *

# Dignity

CERTAIN PEOPLE APPEAR to have dignity. They seem to carry themselves with pride and self-respect. They just look the part. But no matter how undignified a person may look, whether he's homeless, a drunk, or simply without apparent presence, he has a sense of dignity and pride. This is a quality that each manager must recognize, in himself and in others. If we do not recognize our own dignity and that of others, then respect is lost.

In fact, dignity is the reverse side of the quality of respect. Dignity is something you have and don't want damaged. Respect is something you give to others. Even children have dignity. When you show them no respect, it threatens their dignity.

Sometimes one's family gives a person a sense of self-respect. At other times, working for a wonderful organization, or unit, or manager infuses a person with dignity. Crises can also bring true dignity to the surface—the soldier who fights to the end, the manager who refuses to be put down by an unfair boss, even a small nation that refuses to be disregarded—all reflect dignity.

The manager who forgets his own dignity and behaves in ways that cause others to lose regard for him compromises his ability to lead. A sniveling boss, a whining boss, a boss who always has an excuse for not performing, a boss who seeks special privileges he obviously doesn't deserve—all undermine their staffs' respect.

Dignity is not to be confused with pomposity, a puffed-up self-importance. Dignity is not an illusion—or delusion—of grandeur. It is a quality that shines through at all the times, but especially in trying times.

The lessons in this chapter reflect the difficulty in maintaining a sense of dignity and in sensing others' needs for the preservation of their dignity.

## LESSON #66

### The Flip-flop

What can sometimes be worse than moving people around without consulting them is to do it and then change your mind. A director got embroiled in a controversy when he changed a subordinate's direct reporting relationship without talking to her. She just got the message that she was to report to someone else. Feeling resentful, and not being of a mind to sit on that resentment, she presented herself to her former boss and told him precisely how she felt about his treatment of her. Being confronted, he backed down and had her report to him once again.

In the first act of simply transferring this person, the manager had communicated how little he really considered her in his plans. She was treated as if she were an interchangeable part. She was embarrassed and humiliated. Of course, under no conditions should one's reporting relationships be changed without consultation and concurrence from the affected individual.

In this case, the director compounded the problem by caving in and flip-flopping when confronted about his bad form. If the decision wasn't right in the first place, however, the flip-flop makes the whole situation absurd.

The director ended up losing every way he could. The employee, sensing the director's insensitivity, decided she had to leave this director's employ and left the company within three months.

The person who had been her short-lived boss for one day wrote the director off as being wishy-washy, easily intimidated, and as a person who caved in to favorites. The director's vice president heard about the whole mess and removed the director as his backup.

Treating people in ways where they lose face is bad enough without losing one's own dignity by impulsively reversing a decision because of bad form. In this case the director should have apologized to the employee and carefully explained why the move would be of advantage to her and how it would benefit the company. If the original decision was correct, then the issue is only damage control for the offended employee, and that's the kind of thing directors are paid to do.

## LESSON #67

### It's About Time

Does anyone like waiting in a physician's office for an hour, even though having come at the appointed time? Not only doctors but certain airlines think they can get away with using other people's time that way. Many managers do, too. They already know they can't be two places at once—nobody's omnipresent. Yet they set up appointments with two people for the same time or have them backed up sitting in their anterooms because they can't manage their own time.

The result of such thoughtless scheduling is that people are needlessly whiling away their time outside managers' doors, sometimes without even a place to sit. (And there's not even an old copy of *Reader's Digest* to amuse them.) While secretaries, busy with their own work, are forced to play host, the waitees contemplate dark thoughts, such as simply walking away or leaving a nasty note or even fantasizing flinging open the boss's door and saying, "What do you think? I don't have anything to do today?!"

In the end, everyone's time is wasted and the message that is sent throughout the organization (for you know that word will get around) is that a certain manager believes that others are his servants who have nothing better to do than to stand and wait.

The most consistent criticism of a particular general manager was that he had no respect for other people's time. He usually came to the plant at 8:30 or 9:00 A.M. and left around 6:30 or 7:00 P.M. Others came in at 6:30 or 7:00 A.M. and wanted to leave at 4:30 or 5:00 P.M.

On occasion, this general manager would get in later than he intended. As a result, his calendar would be backed up before he'd even arrived, and he would begin seeing people, starting with the earliest scheduled.

He was intense, so his appointments often went beyond the scheduled time limit. He'd also allow outside interruptions to postpone his meetings even further. Often his outer office would be full of people backed up waiting to see him. Sometimes they'd give up and return to their own offices, only to get an irate call from the general manager, "Where are you? I thought we had a meeting!" The result of the constant shifting forward was that people who'd planned to see him at 4:00 P.M. for a half hour were seeing him at 6:00 P.M., bumping their dinner hour or a social engagement.

When the general manager was late for a meeting, which was most of the time, those who came would on some occasions sit and grouse for an hour. They hated to waste the time, but they knew that the general manager would be angry if they weren't present when he showed up.

These actions were interpreted by his staff as inconsiderate behavior. Only *his* time was important! Only *his* personal life was valuable!

There are some managers who make it a habit to be late to meetings where their presence is required. Sometimes they intend to put people in their place. Other times they simply feel that whatever they were doing took precedence over a designated meeting. But that was not the case with this general manager. He simply was a poor manager of his time. His apparent high-handedness came from making himself too accessible, being too involved in detail, and just being a terribly intense person. He intended no putdown.

Such behavior can—and should—be changed. One successful manager never books more than a half hour for each appointment unless the topic demands a major problem-solving session with more than one person. Everyone knows this up front so they are not offended when he announces the meeting is over by rising from his chair.

Your behavior either enhances your staff members' dignity or takes away from it. When you show sensitivity to their commitments and priorities, you'll increase their desire to go the extra mile for you and to make sacrifices in order to meet your requirements or needs. But, if your staff feels that their time and commitments are abused, a resistance to doing anything extra will become their mode of operation. If a change in time is necessary, then get the agreement of the other party.

No one can own time; they can only control their own.

## LESSON #68

### On Being Physical

Some bosses, even those in the higher echelons, get so angry that they become physical. Employees shouldn't put up with a boss that takes a swing at them. Unfortunately, people often do put up with other kinds of physical abuse, such as:

1. The boss who bangs the table causing the colleague to fear for his safety. The boss may know he wouldn't hit him, but how can the colleague know?
2. The boss who blows up and throws furniture against the walls. As one contracts manager said, "I just stood in the corner hoping and praying he'd stop before he hit me."
3. The boss who slams doors or puts his fist through walls causing worry in his colleagues' minds that it could happen to them. This act becomes his primary claim to fame and is a career capper.
4. The boss who throws telephones and desk-top equipment across the room when upset, who himself gets no ulcer but causes everyone else to.
5. The boss who thinks he's the football coach as he pats everyone on the backside, ladies or gentlemen, in a show of, "Go get 'em, fellas."
6. The boss who tells stories about how he beat up a person in a bar when he got fresh with his spouse.
7. The boss who blackmails a colleague through ridicule to play handball, arm wrestle, or run fifteen miles, for the purpose of showing how much of a physical wimp the colleague is.
8. The boss who moves a staff person's office and, "for fun," doesn't tell that person. The boss sees it as a practical joke. The staff member feels violated.

9. The boss who grabs a staff member by the shirt front, saying loudly, "You look at me; I've got something to say to you."

Being physical when you're the boss isn't fair, and in most cases borders on misuse of power and harassment as well as making it clear that you are an ever-present danger to your staff members' health. For such bosses, the rules are simple:

1. Keep your hands to yourself.
2. Leave before you throw anything.
3. Don't drive while you're frustrated.
4. Remember the power differential between you and your staff.
5. Only do to your staff member what you'd do if your boss or your parents were present.

## LESSON #69

### Hazing for Hustle

One small business owner had the habit of hazing new employees with the avowed intent to get them to hustle. He would say quite loudly from thirty feet away, "What have you done for me today, Tom?" Everyone would turn and look at Tom. Some would smile. Some would nonverbally show contempt for the boss. Others would walk on and pay no attention.

Tom would freeze, not knowing what to say. What

was the right answer? Not being a smart aleck himself, and having been warned in any case not to give as good as he got, he simply froze. Inside himself, however, he was writhing with embarrassment.

But this was only the beginning. His boss knew the young man came from a prestigious family. So he'd razz Tom by asking, "Did you eat your cereal with a silver spoon this morning?" or, "Maybe with your daddy's money you could meet your sales quota and never have to see a customer. Ha! Ha!"

This manager felt that goading and embarrassing was a way to motivate. For some people it may work. For Tom, it did not. Indeed, for most people, it never does. Hazing, goading, and personal insults only lead employees to loathe their manager—and in some cases, they may plan to "fix his wagon."

Military academics are well known for allowing hazing of new plebes. These activities are carried out through tradition and within a discipline. While it may be tasteless, it is at least universal and you expect it when you sign on. None of this is true, generally, when one signs up for a job.

Your employees have a right to have you respect their dignity, to show that they are worthy of your esteem. If they aren't, why hire them? Why trip them in public? Why bring them down? Why make them appear worthless? Only so you can rebuild them as they should be to become successful? For some this may work, at some cost to their self-esteem and a new dependence on you, their taskmaster.

Such a process in the civilian world is fraught with legal, moral, motivational, and behavioral consequences. Develop a strategy of tough love if you wish, but preserve the dignity of everyone who works with you. Hazing isn't necessary and may, in fact, undermine the esprit de corps you seek.

## LESSON #70

### Honest Emotion Sometimes Leads to Humiliation

Anger is an honest emotion and, when used cautiously within an already sound work relationship, sets priorities. More often, we blow off steam by overstating our conclusions: "You always avoid going by our sales office," when it may only have happened once or twice.

You, as boss, hold the destiny of an employee in your hands. When you express too much anger, it leads to humiliation, especially if your outburst occurs in the halls, in a meeting, or with your door open. This humiliation in turn leads the employee to resentment, less self-confidence, and sometimes a resume hitting the streets.

One manager developed what he called the quick apology to take care of explosive times when he lost his temper and humiliated a staff person. The staff, however, quickly caught on to this ploy, played the game of "thank you for calling," but became even more wary of this manager's mood swings and manipulation.

Why should they expose themselves to unbridled anger and humiliation if they could avoid it? So the staff move away rather than toward the boss. The result is an uneasy truce and counter-manipulation, not an honest, mutually respectful relationship.

Some managers have come to believe that emotion is to be avoided, and if one is by nature feckless, using anger would appear incongruous, indeed startling. But when you are sincerely put out with performance or attitude, you should express it, but always with the caveats that you aren't going for the kill, you should avoid name-calling, you don't hit below the belt, and you check in with the receiver at a later time to gauge your impact for unintended damage and accuracy of reception.

## LESSON #71

### Dirty Tricks

Fighting dirty can create a feud that may last as long as you stay with your company—and maybe throughout your career. What, then, is fighting dirty?

It's removing a page or an overhead from the packet your opposition has prepared for presentation to higher management.

It's representing your opposition's ideas unfairly in order to distort them and create havoc with their presentation.

Some ambitious managers will go so far as to use character assassination, discrediting a person with vague charges of insubordination or deteriorating competence.

These behaviors and worse are not unusual in

highly politicized organizations. The more ambiguous the company's mission or the higher the level of management, the more potential there is for dirty tricks.

In some organizations, the competition is not from outside competitors but from units within the company. This is especially true, of course, in situations where the company has a monopoly or a 90 percent share of the market.

Don't be naive about those who fight dirty. They are in every organization. Spot them! Assume the worst and neutralize them when possible. Don't, however, become like them. When you lie, cheat, and steal, the other guy wins. Just keep your powder dry and take steps to protect yourself and your staff. To do otherwise is to lose your dignity and descend to the depths of the opposition.

## LESSON #72

### Are We Having Fun Yet?

Tom looked up from his desk and saw Shorty coming in the door, obviously returning from the men's room. He called out, "Hey, Shorty, shouldn't you zip up your fly?" Shorty quickly but clumsily looked down and the whole office burst into laughter. Shorty looked embarrassed as he proceeded to his desk. Even his supervisor was laughing. Are we having fun yet?

Teasing and practical jokes have a place, but when they're used to poke fun at a less-popular person or someone who is disabled, they go too far. This is what can be called hard humor. Teasing doesn't have to be hard humor, however, especially when remarks are made in a trust environment or the humor is at the expense of the person making the remark. For example, when Tom accidentally knocked over his water glass, he said, "If I had a brain I'd play with it."

The worst offenders are bosses. Because they hold the power of job life and death, the victim rarely does more than laugh, too. This hard humor, however, creates anxiety and borders on abuse of power, even when the boss says, "I meant no harm." It can also have severe repercussions.

In one office, a white male manager was standing with a white male supervisor when a young black woman came up to sign a birthday card for a fellow worker. The supervisor feigned holding the card back and said, "No blacks can sign today," and laughed aloud. The manager smiled. The young woman slunk away, but reported the incident. All hell broke loose in the firm. The supervisor was having fun at her expense. The manager was an accomplice. For their behavior, they, along with the whole office, went through sensitivity training.

Don't presume you can have fun at others' expense. It can cause a great loss of dignity in the aggrieved party and can get you in trouble.


## LESSON #73

### Go to the Principal's Office

If you were ever told that the school principal wanted to see you, then you'll understand what follows. People don't like being told, "Come to my office; I want to talk with you." Without an announced subject, you entice the person to revert to a fourth-grade mentality when such a command triggered exaggerated fear. In such a reversion, one loses one's dignity.

One senior manager left word for a middle manager, with whom he constantly argued, to appear at his door the next day at 4:00 P.M. The middle manager was very upset by the time he arrived. He'd worked up a sweat and was ready to walk off the job. But he did appear, feeling quite put-upon and ready for a fight. He sat down, resenting every moment. Then the senior manager told him he was to receive a bonus for saving a large government contract. Further, as a result of his efforts, the customer wanted him as the new program manager, a real career prize.

The resentment that had developed was based upon a previous negative experience with the same senior manager. Such resentment could have been prevented by simple communication that eliminated mystery. The nature of the agenda should *always* be communicated. The manager could have simply said, "I have some good news. Come by my office at 4:00 P.M. tomorrow, if you can." The middle manager would have arrived anticipating pleasure rather than the reverse. If it's bad news, however, that also should be briefly announced in advance.

Why create mystery just because you're the boss? Mysterious requests by authority figures tap into people's insecurities and make them react in childlike ways.

## LESSON #74

### Writing Can Be Wrong

A manager finally had his performance review from his new boss. It was three months late, but very good. The assessment was the most thorough one the manager had ever received. It was also very fair in all aspects. There was criticism, but it was on target and his boss had suggested alternatives. So far so good.

In the past, however, this manager had always been told what actions his boss would take regarding compensation for the next year. In this case it did not happen. So the manager wondered, "When does that take place?"

As time went on, the manager, who'd felt very appreciated for the prior year's efforts, began to wonder what was to happen to his compensation. He'd heard that ranges on his job were to be raised to be more competitive. He knew he was underpaid compared to the market. So he had no doubt that, based on his performance and the change of range, his boss would soon bring him in and tell him what action he was to take.

Ten days later, in a pile of mail, was a letter marked personal and confidential from his boss. He opened the memo and read, "John—your salary for the new year is 6 percent more than last year."

The manager was shocked, first of all at the impersonal way the message was delivered and certainly at the size of the raise, which seemed out of sync with the words of the review.

After cooling his immediate impulse to leave the company, he leveled with his boss at their next regular one-on-one meeting. He didn't attack the boss. He gave him the benefit of the doubt. He did, however, tell him that such an impersonal memo had felt insulting, not rewarding. While not money hungry, he said he'd felt the size of the raise itself was out of line. He did not expect that to change, but he wanted the boss to realize the impact of such a cavalier method of telling him when he saw him almost daily and could have taken him aside.

The written word is a powerful instrument. When used inappropriately or to avoid personal communication, it can bring great harm to a professional relationship. In this case, the offended manager did not let the matter rest with a memo. The offending boss explained that in the interest of time he'd done it this way but now realized it was indeed a poor way to communicate. A better working relationship emerged, with the boss understanding that his manager was a man justly proud of his achievements who wanted to be treated with respect and dignity.

## LESSON #75

### Maintaining Your Dignity

Dignity is internal self-respect that you do not allow to be compromised by the disrespectful actions of others. It is the result of commanding and demanding the respect of others. It derives from taking responsibility for your choices and actions.

Your task or vocation in life has little to do with dignity. Whether you clean toilets or teeth, heal plants or people, manage the mail room or a *Fortune* 500 company, it can be done with dignity. Dignity is in the person, not the job. But how do you command or demand such respect? It is done in the following ways:

1. You're clear what your boundaries are and don't permit them to be consistently violated.
2. You face catastrophe without collapsing.
3. You aren't seduced by temptations that offer false promises.
4. You act on principle, not expedience.
5. You can make tough decisions without making others responsible for your choices.
6. You refuse to submit to experiences you consider degrading.
7. You resist meeting slurs, attacks, and meanness with like behavior.
8. You have high standards and live up to them.

You can also assure your loss of self-respect and dignity in the following ways:

1. You put up with public humiliation by your superiors or colleagues.
2. You behave in "yes, boss" ways to make sure you are your boss's successor.
3. You permit yourself to be pushed beyond your

ethical or business principles for your own or your employer's gain.

4. You allow yourself to be called by your first name while others around you require their last name to be used.

5. You permit your boss to be intrusive.

6. You beg for something you want.

7. You take yourself so seriously that others think you are pompous and mockable.

8. You become a whining victim of life and its circumstances.

9. You act out of fear of job loss, telling the truth, conflict, failure, or rejection.

Commanding and demanding respect will serve those you work with or supervise in wonderful ways. Genuine dignity is often heroic to those who witness it. When you act with dignity and self-respect, you become a model for others. You can almost singlehandedly create an environment where people treat each other as persons of dignity. Such a workplace is an environment where people grow in maturity, self-confidence, and the ability to take on tougher and more challenging tasks, which is the goal of every thinking company.

# CHAPTER EIGHT

\*

# Integrity

INTEGRITY MEANS, IN essence, to be integrated, to have your psychological, spiritual, intellectual, ethical, and social parts congruent with one another. An integrated manager lets the right hand know what the left is doing. An integrated manager doesn't speak out of both sides of his mouth. He doesn't espouse always being honest and aboveboard, then suggest that in order to do business in Swaziland, "We'll have to use bribes." If bribing is okay, then always being honest and aboveboard is not.

Lying or asking your people to lie, telling different stories in different places but still in front of one's staff, or blatantly cheating on expenses with full knowledge of one's staff—all undermine the belief that others have in your integrity.

When you show a lack of integrity and double-deal a customer or another unit in your organization, your staff think, "When will he do it to us?"

Remarkably, some managers don't ever under-

stand the concept of integrity. Beating the other
fellow by any means sends the message that you
have no core, no center.

The quality of integrity has some potential benefit
and some potential pain for the manager. The benefits are that on value issues you'll be predictable.
You won't have to create policies and procedures
to cover every contingency. Your staff will know
what to do when sticky decisions or delicate choices
must be made. Customers and colleagues will know
that your word is your bond, and deals will stay in
place.

The pain will come when holding to a core principle personally costs you. Sometimes it's a piece of
business you wanted. Sometimes it's a promotion
you'd have received for simply keeping your mouth
shut. Sometimes it's losing a commission when you
point out a mistake on a billing. Whatever the issue,
your advantage is lost because you were honorable.
But that is how you know you have integrity.

Integrity doesn't mean rigidity, but it does mean
holding dear in every way the various parts of your
personality and your life.

The following lessons illustrate times that integrity truly matters.

## LESSON #76

### "We Are Not Amused"

Everyone knew exactly what Queen Victoria
meant when she uttered those words. She meant

that she, the royal personage, representing all that was proper throughout the British Empire, was highly displeased. Today, when a manager who wants to put down a cocky or unrepentant staff member begins a sentence with "We think—" "We believe—" or uses some other collective pronoun, sometimes he's really speaking for himself.

By using the plural, the manager implies that the president, the firm's vice presidents, God, the angel Gabriel, and all the archangels, not just him, are really upset. What the employee infers is that the manager doesn't have the courage to let his staff person know exactly what *he* thinks about some behavior, that this manager is actually intimidated by someone who reports to him. At worst, the staff member sees fear in the manager's eyes—the fear of dealing face-to-face. At best—let's face it—he sees a pompous ass.

True authority in interpersonal relations is best achieved when you are the author of your own demands, feelings, and opinions. It evokes a desire in the other person to please that the phrase *we want* never does. After all, it should indeed be the staff member who wants to please you.

When you say *we,* you are speaking for people not present, which can be rather presumptuous. By using *I,* you convey a sense of responsibility. It signals that you are willing to be held accountable for what you are saying, which sets a good model for all your staff (imagine *everyone* saying *we*). Using *I* develops credibility and honesty, mandatory for all leaders. Say "I think—" "I believe—" "I want—" or "I expect—" and then add your observations. The staff member cares much more for what *you* think than for a collection of *we*'s.

## LESSON #77

### Owning Up

For several hours the hunting party had wandered in circles. Now that night was coming on, it was obvious that they were lost. Threatening storm clouds were racing toward them.

"You said you were the greatest guide in Canada," one of the irate hunters shouted at the guide.

"I am," the guide said, "but I think we wandered into Minnesota about four hours ago!"

The guide wouldn't admit his mistake, even after it was obvious to everyone. Because of him, they faced the almost certain prospect of no success and a wet, uncomfortable night in the woods. The hunters made two conclusions: that they had an incompetent guide and to never follow him again.

As a manager, you are a guide for your organization. You don't have to wait until faced with an unpleasant night in the woods to recognize that a wrong turn, a poor decision, or a missed signal has occurred.

Do you ever say, "I was wrong," or "I blew it," or "You are right?" What do you say when a staff member proves you took the wrong turn, picked the wrong alternative, selected the wrong product, or promoted the wrong person? How you answer guides your subordinates to a number of decisions.

Managers with integrity freely admit their mistakes. By doing so, they save their organization countless hours of misdirected work and avoid unnecessary rework. Managers who appropriately prepare, read signals, and promptly change course do two things: First, they prove they're competent to lead the group. They listen. They don't let their egos block the process. They demonstrate by their actions that they can be influenced. They earn the respect of their working teams by consistently guiding them to the right objective. Second, such managers demonstrate confidence in themselves and their sources of information.

Nothing builds up an organization more than the knowledge that the boss will change a decision because of something a subordinate discovered.

## LESSON #78

### P/A Relationships

P/A organizations are those where passive-aggressive relationships are the norm. All relationships have some passive-aggressive qualities. A smile may hide anger. Apparent agreement to a fully discussed plan may, in fact, be only an act. Congratulations on a success may be a facade covering jealousy or vindictiveness.

If people relate to each other in a primary mode of passive-aggressiveness, you'll find:

- Excessive behind-the-scenes maneuvering
- Complaints to third parties, rather than to the person being complained about
- Withholding of negative expressions of fear or anger
- Complying maliciously
- Poking fun at those not present
- Nonacceptance of responsibility by individuals
- Revenge behavior (getting even, rather than getting mad)
- Negative fantasies or a proliferation of *If only* thoughts, both expressed or unexpressed
- Believing worst-case reports
- Vicious, personally destructive rumor mills
- Unrealistic expectations of authority figures
- Fruitless overly polite public meetings

Such organizations lack integrity, or wholeness, because they are neurotic. What is projected as reality is not what's really going on.

Sometimes you can make an organization behave in passive-aggressive ways all by yourself. You can do it through abrasive, shoot-the-messenger, insulting, punishing, or threatening remarks, observations, and orders. Everyone dives for the trenches—or leaves—in the face of such behavior.

Individuals with a passive-aggressive emotional style may also be attracted to organizations, often incorporating the helping professions, that value overt behavior that only emphasizes such qualities as empathy, dependence, warmth, intimacy, and cooperation. By emphasizing these so-called love derivatives, they deemphasize the derivatives of anger, which include competition, independence, aggression, and conflict. Anger is seen as wrong, so it can only be expressed indirectly. Thus we have a P/A organization, for example, where it is a sin to admit that your own self-interest is motivating you.

Some of us can live in P/A organizations because they match our psychological profile. Some of us are in P/A institutions and should leave before we become like them. Some of us are in a position to help P/A organizations change to greater organizational integrity, where what you see is what you get. The task is difficult and requires time, patience, and often outside consultants who aren't caught up in the P/A dynamic.

The first place to look for who's causing the lack of corporate integrity is in yourself. Reform such behavior by starting with your own. If you can't, then move to an organization where what you see is really what you get. Only in that place will you be able to retain your integrity.

## LESSON #79

### Truth or Consequences

Two aerospace contractors wanted to turn around a situation of miscommunication between them that also involved their customer, the U.S. Navy. They brought in a consultant who, after extensive interviews with employees of both companies and the navy, found this scenario.

Prior to the contract award, Contractor 1 had told Contractor 2 that this would be an equal partnership. After signing the contract, Contractor 1 reneged, denying they'd ever agreed to that. They further told the navy they'd been working on the contract for three months when they hadn't, because they were short of cash. Contractor 1 also told Contractor 2 that they could have certain subcontracts and then farmed them out behind Contractor 2's back. In program reviews for the navy, Contractor 1 would report progress that hadn't been accomplished and would cover up technical problems that they hoped to fix before they were discovered. They expected Contractor 2 to corroborate the lies. Contractor 2, in the meantime, decided that they'd been toyed with, so, even though denying it to Contractor 1, they had their own marketing people in the navy's program office badmouth Contractor 1. The commander-in-charge had become completely overwhelmed, because it soon became obvious to his admiral that the commander himself had either been lying or was incompetent.

A few early lies to get advantage or to cover lack of progress turned a $400 million contract into a debacle of distrust, fear, and suspicion that each new generation of program managers inherited. Thus, no matter how many new people the navy, Contractor 1, or Contractor 2 put on the program, distrust continued.

We all are tempted to lie at some time, but it seldom pays, especially in the workplace. And it never pays in the long run. Also, lying in front of your staff, your boss, or others in the company, if they know or suspect it to be a lie, places those individuals in a position of collusion, without giving them the opportunity to decide if they wish to be in that position, just as Contractor 1 did to Contractor 2.

It also doesn't pay to ask your staff to veil or distort information that belongs to the company. In some companies, managers talk of doing "rain dances for the Tower," which conveys the image of stories about the future that are larger than life. Rain dances, however, only produce more rain dances. Once every level does it for their superiors, real communication is lost.

Your subordinates, of course, have no obligation to lie for you, your department, or your division. They don't belong to you, and threatening them with the loss of their jobs is taking unfair advantage of your position.

## LESSON #80

### Machiavelli's Corrupting Qualities

One manager was known as the master manipulator. When you met with him or his people, the question always was, what's their game this time? As the director of marketing, he might want engineering to commit to a resource allocation against a phony projection. Or he might be lining up the business area team to cover his mistakes with a customer until it was too late for the customer to go to another vendor. No matter how straight you might be, this manager would soon create a situation for you that had no positive choice, and you would find yourself in a moral Catch-22.

Machiavellian managers will come through the keyhole or over the transom even when the door is unlocked. They enjoy the game of corrupting their team and out-strategizing the other person, even when it's not to their long-term advantage or to the advantage of the company.

When you demand that your people concoct positions you hope will rig relationships in your favor with other departments, customers, suppliers, or competitors rather than revealing what you or your organization really believe, you corrupt. You develop a cynicism among others and create a climate of disgust and double-dealing that ultimately works against your interests. For eventually, your lessons will be learned all too well by others, and they will turn their corrupting skills on you.

## LESSON #81

### Decisions, Decisions

Some managers like clear-cut alternatives presented by their staffs. "Give me a problem," they say, "but also give me alternative approaches to solving the problem." This manager was definitely not that way. He was never pleased to be put in a position where he had to choose. If his staff provided clear alternatives, they would be berated for not doing their job.

Realizing that their manager felt cornered when having to make a choice, his staff learned to create work that presented no clear alternatives but simply an analysis of the situation. But when given no clear choices, he would say, "Why is it you force me to do everything myself?"

As a manager, it is your job to make decisions—to choose. And it is your staff's job, if you have trained them well, to present you with the best alternatives that allow you to make the best choices. If you discourage your staff from doing this or send them confusing signals, then what you will get will be confusing information that will not lead to any intelligent decision at all.

## LESSON #82

### Cleaning Up the Garbage

Human nature being what it is, most people seem to like gossip—the juicier the better. Who's getting a divorce? Who's sleeping with whom? Who's a dollar short and a day late? It's sort of a substitute for true intimacy, but it's never innocent. When people gossip to you about colleagues, they have reasons. Lest we forget, all corporate behavior is purposeful.

Gossips are everywhere. They look for garbage. They create it. They pass it on. They are at the water coolers, in the washrooms, and at the company picnic or Christmas party. They drop hints to your spouse about how you goof off or how so-and-so would like to take you home. They repeat any rumor with little pursuit of truth. When they find a like-minded soul, they spend intimate hours together taking others apart.

What can you do with these gossips? Assuming you can resist your own desire to pick through corporate garbage—realizing there really is very little you can gain from that activity—then the best approach is being straight with others. If you are normally open with people, you'll get direct information and not the company's trash.

Participating in direct action is not what a gossiper particularly has in mind. When given gossip, the best action is to ask innocently, "Why are you telling me this?" or, better yet, "What do you think, I, or we, should do with this information?" Soon you will find yourself less of a garbage can, will be respected for your style, and will miss absolutely nothing except garbage that can't be recycled.

## LESSON #83

### A Few Words on Your Boss's Competence: Don't

It's been a pleasant lunch. It's not often you get invited to chat with your boss's boss, and the conversation has been enjoyable, friendly. You're a little loosened up. You've asked him questions about the division's profits and his new summer home; he's asked about your good work on the McFarland project and your vacation plans. Then, casually, comes another question: "Say, Sam, do you think Tom [your boss] is really able to do this job? You've been working with him for a year now."

Now what, you think. Do you tell the truth? There are some positive things to emphasize. But, then, again, there are those negatives.

The real question is, is it your place to give a performance review of your boss in such an informal setting?

The answer is almost always *no*. Well, that's *almost* always, because sometimes, regardless of whether the setting is formal or informal, the staff member should blow the whistle for everyone's good. Your boss may be an alcoholic who needs help because he's missing work, not making decisions, drinking in the office; or he may be involved with illegal acts or activities that are serious violations of company policy.

Generally speaking, though, it seems very bad form to be drinking your third martini and giving your boss's boss an earful on your supervisor's competence. Still, you've been asked a direct question, and you have to say something. Being straightforward—and tactful, of course—helps.

"You flatter me, Joe, to ask my opinion of Tom. But I'm sure you understand the difficulty of discussing my boss in a setting such as this, especially if I don't say the same thing to him before I say it to someone else," or, "Gee, Joe, I don't think Tom would think kindly of me giving you an off-the-record opinion. Do you?"

In other words, you decline the opportunity, aware of being seduced by your boss's boss. He may be using you for his own ends or testing you to see how you react in such situations. He may simply have had one too many himself and tomorrow may regret having asked you for your opinion. While it may seem flattering to become the confidant of your boss's boss, there lurks danger that can only lead you into deeper political games. Most of the time it's better to beg off in a tactful way. But if for some extremely important reason you must wisely and honestly discuss such sensitive matters, make the potential benefit exceed the great risk you are taking.

What if, though, your boss's incompetence is so overwhelming that you are thinking of leaving the company? If you can, it is always better to tell your boss that you can't continue as is and you have to talk to his boss about some career opportunities. Quietly telling that person that you are leaving because you can't work with your boss shows respect for your boss's boss and the company. Now the issue is you, not the boss. You are preparing to leave, and the company should have the option to try to keep you.

## LESSON #84

### Hidden Versus Surface Team Agendas

We often use the expression *hidden agenda* as if it implied a bad thing. The truth is that hidden agendas are neither better nor worse than surface agendas except where hidden personal agendas are the primary driver of an organization's relationships. Even if it were possible, hidden agendas shouldn't all be surfaced, for all of us have some that wouldn't be acceptable to someone but are ultimately harmless. However, where they undermine the credibility or progress of a process, they undermine the integrity of those who are acting in open and committed ways.

We can guess there are hidden agendas in teams when there seems to be a lack of progress that is unexplainable by ordinary observation. Sometimes nonverbal signals—such as covert exchanges, apparent boredom, or consistent blocking of action—hint of their existence.

There are three types of hidden agendas within any work team: those of the team members, those of the team leaders, and those between an individual member and the team, whether conscious or unconscious.

Team members:

- May have hip-pocket solutions
- May represent hidden constituents
- May have divided loyalties
- May fear personal consequences
- May hold unexpressed resentment
- May belong to competing coalitions

Team leaders:

- May desire to cut the throat of an obstreperous member

- May have a hip-pocket solution
- May be protecting favorite people
- May be secretly biased on a solution
- May want to postpone but aren't saying so
- May feel their power is threatened
- May want to leave early but haven't said so

Individual members:

- May be competing for influence with the team leader
- May hold conscious or unconscious hostility toward the leader
- May resent feeling dependent on the leader
- May feel passive toward a dominant leader
- May support hip-pocket solutions or previous collusion of the leader and other team members

There are three actions that you should take to make sure a team is adhering to the integrity of its purpose:

1. *Always* be aware of hidden agendas that have an impact on progress. Realize that both surface and hidden agendas are always present.
2. If not *too* embarrassing to a particular individual, when in a group, stop the group's fumbling and diagnose the hidden agenda that's blocking progress. Discuss it, clarify the issue if possible, then move on.
3. Never scold the holders of hidden agendas, except where the hidden agendas are so dominant that integrity has been compromised.

## LESSON #85

### Promises, Promises

Some years ago, a problem developed in a functionally organized division of a large company. The problem was that people weren't meeting their agreed-upon deadlines.

Deadlines were very important to this division because it was a low-cost, high-volume production house. Competition was tough, and customers were demanding. The sales force therefore often agreed to what appeared to the engineering and production departments as unfair and impossible. Inventories were expensive. Rusted parts increased waste. It was devastating to budgets to have people standing idle. The cash flow was affected when deliveries weren't made. When deadlines weren't met, customers were encouraged to find second sources or to order the next generation of products from another company. Everyone in the division knew these facts, but still deadlines weren't met. The entire division had lost its integrity.

Through interviews, two major causes of the problem emerged. First, the culprits were as plain as the nose on your face—they were always the other guys. Engineering reported receiving poor specs and constant changes from marketing so that it couldn't design properly. Marketing expressed frustration with the customer, who wasn't clear about what he wanted, so constant change orders were necessary. Production complained that it often received a design from engineering that it couldn't make. According to manufacturing, procurement wasn't ordering parts early enough so that they could hold inventory down. No one was even trying to be fair to the other departments but were only interested in defending themselves.

The second cause was that people were simply lying about their ability to meet deadlines. In program reviews, a program manager might produce colorful charts that showed milestones, costs to complete, and shipping dates that were fictional. Everyone on the program knew it. The same team had met for two difficult hours before they went to the general manager's review; knowing that the truth wasn't going to be acceptable, they made promises they just couldn't keep.

If all parties were actually seeking to be fair to others, teamwork could emerge, and together they could get the job done. But with everyone pointing fingers at others while defending themselves, the organization simply gridlocked. An unstated collusion developed in which everyone lived a lie to protect themselves.

It is important that a manager teach staff members early in the relationship that fixing blame on others and doing rain dances creates a lack of personal and organizational integrity that undermines success. Deadlines, commitments, and promises are to be kept or renegotiated. Never avoid, procrastinate, hedge, or blame others unfairly.

Of course, the best way to teach your staff about

meeting deadlines and commitments and fulfilling promises is for you to do the same and not to use others as an excuse. Your integrity then sets the pace for others. The work of many people in your organization is dependent upon those who manage, and they must be the plumb line for others.

# CHAPTER NINE

\*

# Candor

MANAGERS WHO VERBALLY abuse, insult, threaten, and intimidate their associates on purpose would appear to have been abused when young, either at work or in their families. Otherwise, why would they believe that extreme anger, acted out, could have a long-term positive effect? One employee said, "Yell at me once; the next time you have to hunt for me." Employees, vendors, and certainly customers want no part of a person who consistently invades their space and screams and carries on in what amounts to tantrums. But many such behaviors go on and are often subtly approved by the company. Often they fly under the banner of being "brutally honest."

Managers can get reputations for not just being insensitive but for scolding, shaming, or dressing down employees in front of others, for berating their teams, using sarcasm, and belittling to motivate. They carry those reputations for a lifetime of work, and just a few such stories is all that it takes to handicap a person's career.

But, you might say, there are senior managers who've gotten ahead with these tactics. Today, however, there are fewer successful bullies, although some entrepreneurs feel they own their employees and therefore can kick them around. At the same time, we have to realize that some managers may just see themselves as tough and may believe that people respect them for their no-nonsense attitude. They are often surprised to discover just how frightening they are to the people around them.

Some managers assume that people are like jackasses, needing carrots and sticks, particularly sticks, to make them move. So when they lose their temper, they believe it motivates people. Indeed it may, but when the manager isn't present, entropy quickly sets in and the people plod until the next carrot or stick appears.

Expressing feelings is a good thing. People need to know the real priorities of a manager and often it's necessary to express these strongly. However, rather than using "brutal honesty" where the manager shows little assessment of his or her impact, the ideal quality is one of expressing "caring candor."

Caring candor is descriptive rather than punitive. It's a quality in managers that causes them to worry about the loss of face by a person needing to be told of his shortcomings.

While the truth is conveyed using caring candor, such candor is also used to heighten awareness, awaken new commitment, create more energy, and bestow employees with a desire to learn. When the person leaves your office, he should not feel diminished. He should not feel hatred for himself, his job, or you.

Finally, "brutal honesty" may be cosmetic words used to cover a certain sadistic streak in a manager. He uses the imbalance of power to gain personal satisfaction from hurting another person. While this is a dark thought, it is quite within the realm of possibility.

If you must lose your temper, lose it while still caring about the impact of your words. If you must express your frustrations, do it knowing you want the person with whom you're speaking to rise to greater achievements. If you must give feedback that is critical, don't give it from a position that hangs a person, then gives them a "fair trial." Use caring candor.

This chapter gives examples where lessons about caring candor can be learned.

## LESSON #86

### It's a Dirty, Rotten, Crummy Job, but Somebody's Gotta Do It

There are tasks that every manager has to assign that are simply dirty work. They may be routine, mundane duties such as coordinating the blood bank donors or leading this year's United Way campaign, and the person chosen to carry out these jobs may look on them as downgrading. Sometimes the task, though part of a necessary company program, is tough and thankless with negative aspects that it's tempting for a supervisor to disguise with hyperbolic language and little candor.

When making assignments like these, the only thing you can do is be candid. It's just a task, and someone has to do it. It's a necessary task, however, so you don't have to minimize its contribution to the company. At the same time, be careful you don't puff it out of proportion, making wild promises (or bribes) to get someone to accept the assignment.

There are also major assignments that don't align with a person's career path. An engineer, for example, might be asked to detour from his career goals to take on a tough program or to go to an overseas assignment for two or three years, but be promised the moon when the program is over. This happens constantly, and rarely are the promises able to be kept. Sometimes the sponsoring vice president is moved to another spot and unable to act on the promise. Or it may be that the company's need for the skills of the person on special assignment are no longer needed. At other times, management is simply exploiting the person without taking his needs into consideration. After leading two or three special programs, the engineer will view such promises with skepticism. He will know that when the program is over, his prospects for picking up his chosen career path may be very limited or nonexistent.

The more honest we can be about assignments, the better. People mind making personal sacrifices less when they are being treated as adults

and included in the reasoning process. They do
dislike being treated as fools or made to feel
as if they are being successfully tricked by the
assignor.

## LESSON #87

### Memos We Never Finished Reading

TO: All Directors
FROM: Office of the Corporate Secretary
RE: Annual Meeting

Be that as it may and as a gregarious society, your interest and participation is a vital
and primordial aspect of The Company. Thus
it is that you are reminded of the forthcoming
Annual Meeting with its germane aspects. . . .

By now, you're probably totally obfuscated and
wondering why the writer can't elucidate. (Then
again, you may simply be *confused* and wondering
why the writer can't *be clear!*) This use of flowery
language is an unnecessary burden in today's business environment.

We all have too much to read. When we read anything that appears to use three words when one will
do, we soon lose interest. Some of this we can't control, like articles that we need to read for our work,
but we can certainly improve our own memos.

First, we have to remind ourselves that memos

shouldn't be used as the primary form of communication, only as confirmation or for background. That should help cut down on quite a few. When memos are necessary, some basic rules can help keep them simple and clear:

1. Make your communication as short as possible.
2. Keep the concepts simple and to the point.
3. Keep your language concrete and Anglo-Saxon.
4. Avoid Latin-based words such as *obfuscate* and *elucidate*.
5. Write to express, not to impress.
6. Make it your goal to write so well that the receiver will welcome your memos as a breath of fresh air and will look forward to receiving them.
7. Don't *ever* use memos to blast, insult, name-call, or subtly or sarcastically, even euphemistically, put down the receiver. Such misuse of candor can come back to haunt you.

Simple guidelines to remember: After all, memos can be copied. Some even find their way into books.

## LESSON #88

### Just Between You and I

Your associate has just said, "I believe either her or I has to go to the meeting." What do you say about misusing the pronoun *her* for *she*? At a later date he says, "I should have went instead of you." Now what do you say, especially if you aren't close to the person and don't have an arrangement where you can give feedback of a somewhat personal nature? People have lost contracts because of misspelled words in the proposal. Able managers are passed over for positions of more responsibility because of bad grammar.

The truth is that poor English grammar in someone expected to speak in the American tongue tends to be a career-limiting circumstance. It is really not just a personal issue, it is a performance issue. English, both written and spoken, is important to getting the job done not only in the United States but globally. Poor English almost certainly will undermine credibility in short-term business affairs. Long-term, it may have the same effect, although deeper knowledge of a person's competencies may overcome the English deficit.

Unfortunately, once we get beyond our preparatory years and our parents' influence, few people will take on the uncomfortable task of correcting our English. That task then falls to caring colleagues. But be kind! Increasingly, you may be correcting someone for whom English is a second language. Or it may be someone who is overly sensitive and thinks the use of such a phrase as *between you and I* sounds more elegant, when in fact, it's simply wrong. Take your associate or staff member aside as soon as the misuse occurs and quote back to him what he said. He may not realize he is missing the tense or the voice, for example, and simply needs the slip pointed out. In some instances he just may not know any better.

## LESSON #89

### When to Say You're Sorry

Knowing when to apologize may seem on the surface to be simply a matter of etiquette. That's true if you're apologizing for bumping into a coffee-holding patron in the company cafeteria. Failing to apologize, however, when through your actions real harm has been done, such as alienating a colleague's customer, builds ill will, a bad reputation, and often a negative, uncooperative attitude from the aggrieved person.

Most better business organizations know that if a customer has been insulted, he first wants an apology. It's the beginning of a talk that can then result in satisfying the customer's needs. The apologizer loses no face, and customer satisfaction is increased. An apology is a way to neutralize bad feelings so that the substance of the dispute can be put on the table to be addressed. The words aren't enough, however; one has to mean them.

If you gave the wrong specifications to the vendor, even though it wasn't entirely your doing, when you realize the negative consequence to the vendor, at least say—and mean—"I'm sorry."

If you're late going home and your spouse is angry because a hot dinner was spoiled, don't say, "If you only knew how hard it was to get home even at this time." Simply say, "I'm sorry."

One of the travesties of social intercourse today

is when, after a two-hour unexplained wait on the tarmac, the airline pilot says, "Thank you for your patience." Not, "I'm sorry," just thanks for your patience. The fact is you weren't patient, and you are still fuming.

There is something magical about candidly owning up and saying the magic words, "I'm sorry," and meaning them.

## LESSON #90

### Do Your Leveling Best

No one likes to be confronted. For many, it's hard to confront. But how many times do we want to—when an associate doesn't perform, when a staff member says something stupid, when your boss blows it, or when a customer demands the impossible.

Confrontation always includes your speaking of the other person's behavior in some judgmental fashion. For example, "You talked too much"; "You shouldn't have said what you said (or did what you did)"; "You were unethical"; "How stupid can one person be! You drove off the customer"; "You say impossible things." What can the result be but defensiveness on the part of the accused, even if they feel the charge is correct?

Why not give them some room? Don't confront, level! For example: "John, do you realize the impact on me when we don't deliver what I said we would?" or "Joan, when you say things to the customer about later delivery, it scares me to death!" or "When you tell me we can't make deliveries, I begin to question whether we ever really had a deal." This is called leveling. It's where you talk about the impact on you of the other person's behavior. The other person may say, "That's your problem," or "How dumb can you be," but odds are that the person is stuck with explaining why he screwed up rather than explaining why you're imperceptive. The next time that person will be more careful. Your customer will realize you're a person. Your staff will know you have impact. How can you lose when you take the risk to level?

## LESSON #91

### "May I Be Brutally Honest?"

Brutal honesty may never be appropriate except in life-and-death situations. When in an airplane getting ready to crash, when a disease takes a turn for the worse, or when someone truly has hurt you to the point where you must let them know what they've done or stay away from them, then brutal honesty may be necessary.

Most circumstances demand caring candor. Caring candor is the necessary mode when your spouse asks your opinion about what you consider to be an awful tie or a bad hairdo, or a staff member has little respect for the boss.

One Texas executive said in a meeting, "What we need is brutal honesty," yet she proved to be the most vulnerable person on the team to the brutal effects of total honesty. She really wanted caring candor or consideration of the potential impact of criticism, especially on her. Caring candor is honesty with concern about the impact on another.

When giving feedback to an associate, it means speaking to specific behaviors that are of concern to you and others. It means worrying about the possible loss of face by the receiver of the feedback so that such feedback is done carefully and not in front of others who might mock the person afterward. It means conveying that "the future can be better than today" for the person to whom you speak. It means offering to help, not abandoning the other person to fate's whimsy.

## LESSON #92

### *Caveat ad Hominem*

Most of us can be cowards about certain things. Instead of having a heart-to-heart talk with a staff member or even our spouse, we use zingers to criticize, and we do this most often when we have an audience.

"As usual, Marj doesn't have the letter ready"— said in front of a client.

"Well, Fred, I guess we'll have another fiasco that we can't control. Seems like it's the usual thing these days!"—said in front of the whole staff, of course.

"Mary's getting ready, but the dog could die while

she puts on her makeup"—said in front of friends who've come to take you out to dinner.

Zingers as replacements for candidness are used to cut people down, or stir them up to fight back, to communicate the negative while avoiding the consequences, or perhaps to straighten them out. Rarely do any of these results occur. Subordinates can't fight back without jeopardizing their jobs or, even worse, having their boss say in front of others, "Don't be so thin-skinned." Staff members lose if they keep still, and they lose if they complain.

This zapping behavior achieves nothing. To use such phrases is to indulge in ad hominems, which literally means *to the person,* not to the issue or the problem. It's one thing to say, "There isn't enough backup data in the proposal." It's quite another to impugn the proposer's commitment by saying, "If you'd get off your backside and not be so lazy, your proposals would be complete." The first is a straight-forward candid observation that can be discussed. The second is simply an insult that stimulates defensiveness and will not produce what you need.

Even subtle insults have unusual impact. Just because staff members don't fold up and burst into tears doesn't mean that they haven't been affected. Insulting phrases will long be remembered by the person to whom they're said. They will cause that person to say, "If I can't get mad, at least I can get even!"

So the next time you feel yourself about to lash out at a staff member, stop and rephrase what you have to say in such a way that the issue, not the person, can be discussed. Then in a way that shows you think about your impact, directly state your critique or point of view. Otherwise you'll end up with staff who feel bad about themselves, bad about you, bad about the job and, perhaps, just mad enough to get even.

## LESSON #93

### Delivering a Compliment

Because many people have poor or damaged self-images, they're generally suspicious of compliments, especially when they seem uncalled-for from the giver. "Why would he tell me that?" "What does she want?" In addition, many of us stumble over giving sincere and candid compliments for fear of appearing weak or maybe even giving the other person the upper hand. So here are some ways to at least advance the candor and credibility of your well-meaning comments:

1. Tell others what you specifically liked. For example, don't say, "You do good work, John." Say, "You really turned that customer around, John."
2. Avoid putting thorns on the roses you hand out. Don't say, "Mary, more customers speak warmly of you now that you've lost that fifty pounds."
3. Avoid double entendres with anyone with whom you aren't *very* close. Avoid them especially in front of strangers or large management groups. In groups, coded communication turns others off or leaves them confused. So beware of, "Let me

introduce you to the least helpful, dumbest, most expensive consultant I know." Translated, it may well mean, "This guy is the best you'll ever see and the most secure to let me insult him." These statements can backfire badly.

4. When you give a compliment, you be the one to give it. None of this *me, too* stuff. If you've overlooked a subordinate's good work and your boss compliments her first, shame on you, but don't compound it by saying, "I feel the same."

5. Don't praise people if you're not being so complimentary behind their backs. Word gets back and incredulity sets in.

6. Just as children hate to be compared with their playmates, so adults hate to be complimented with comparisons. For example, "You are faster than many other computer programmers in this office" may be received as a mixed blessing. The person is left wondering what you were trying to tell him.

7. Avoid adding tails to your compliments. When you say, "Now, this report is beautifully laid out, but—" you are sending mixed messages.

8. The *if only* compliment, while intended to motivate employees, can also turn them off, especially if they feel they're already performing in excess of your expectations. So don't say, "You have the ability to be a really outstanding supervisor, if you would just get tougher with people."

In conclusion:

1. Compliment directly, not through others.
2. If you can't give a compliment without a lot

of extra *if only* noise, don't give it.

3. Do it in writing. The receiver then knows you weren't passing a casual comment.
4. Give it consistently and sincerely, or you may be seen as being nice only to get what you want when you need it.
5. Finally, when you receive praise, simply say, "Thank you." None of this "Oh, I don't deserve it," or "You shouldn't thank me." Only if others are clearly being left out should you say, specifically, who else should be recognized.

In other words, don't reject positive strokes sincerely given, and don't offer them unless they are sincerely given.

## LESSON #94

### Candor Without Context

Sometimes we talk of interpersonal skills as if they are tools one uses in changing a tire. Being candid in such a way as to have the other person appreciate it depends not only on the skill of the giver but also greatly on the context in which the candor is expressed. No matter how effective you are at communicating with caring candor, the preexisting nature of the relationship is extremely important to the success of the candid exchange.

Let's say it's your job to tell a subordinate that he is being laid off. The truth is that this person is the least skilled of your people and you must cut one person from your group. How candid can you be?

If you have had a previously open relationship where your staff member felt you sincerely cared about him, then you can sit down and tell him that he is to be laid off and why. The staff member may be unhappy, but he will listen as you go further to coach him on how to upgrade his skills, perhaps suggesting training or educational institutions that would be most appropriate.

On the other hand, if there is a preexisting fear on the part of the staff member that leads him to be suspicious of whatever you say, then your candor and inclination of personal interest will be suspect. Your candor may in this case be seen as punishing, cruel, or probably a misrepresentation of the facts. In other words, the kind of relationship you have with the person means a great deal.

The manager who believes that it is important to be completely candid at all times with everybody puts the burden on the receiver to factor in the manager's lack of skill and sensitivity to the circumstances. He may proudly announce he's always honest, telling it like it is. This simply means he plans to be insensitive to the context in which the candor takes place.

For certain cultures, such as Japan's, the context is everything. The two key factors in the Japanese transaction are : (1) Is the person of greater or lesser rank? and (2) Are they really in and of my group? Those two factors affect what is said by whom and to whom.

Americans have contextual concerns similar to those of the Japanese, but these are generally denied as key factors. You know this is true when a staff member says, "Who the heck does he think he is?" That's the contextual issue.

Ideally, all of our working relationships should provide a supportive context for an exchange marked by candor. Since you know that's not possible, you have to take the relationship into account when you choose the level of candor you'll use with your boss, your colleagues, your staff, your customers, or whoever you come in contact with.

## LESSON #95

### "Gotcha"

A young boy was living with his grandmother during the depression. As he returned home from school one day, he was pleased to see that his mother had come to visit. As they chatted, she asked him if he had complied with the rule never to permit another child to ride on his bike with him. He lied and assured her he was in full compliance, not knowing that she'd just seen him drop a friend off two blocks from home. He was sent outside to cut a switch for his punishment. His paddling was interrupted four times as one by one the frail switches broke and he was required to return outside to cut another. No one was happy during this event, especially not the young boy.

What happened, of course, is that he was trapped,

put in a position where he had to make an embarrassing confession or tell a lie. He decided on the latter. Either approach would have brought on the switch.

The story is similar to the type of situation that often happens in an organization. The boss knows a staff member has not met a commitment, has done something against instructions, or has simply procrastinated. The boss then puts the staff member in a position of having to make one of two decisions—either to make an embarrassing confession, which would result in criticism and perhaps abuse, or to lie, which is uncomfortable for all concerned. Sometimes the latter seems to be the least painful course for the staff member, at least initially.

If you as the boss know something, however, immediately lay it on the line in a caring as well as candid way so that other people come out of the situation with their self-regard intact and with renewed vigor to show you and themselves what they can do. Perhaps commitments made were unreal, given other tasks. Perhaps you asked too much. Perhaps the staff members are poor at managing time and priorities and need your help. Now's the time.

If you trap people once or twice, they'll begin to find ways to avoid such traps and will give you less and less information, which hardly leads to the candid environment you would like to create.

# CHAPTER TEN

## *

# Responsiveness

I LIKE WEBSTER'S definition of responsiveness: "reacting easily or readily to suggestion or appeal." Another definition might be, "closing the communication loop." Both imply positive, meaningful, and productive working relationships.

When a manager is considered unresponsive, he may be described as a procrastinator, someone who says yes but lacks follow-through. Procrastination can destroy relationships and wreck companies. So, whether it's being on time, making calls or decisions, writing reports, doing paperwork, billing clients, confronting when necessary, paying a compliment, asking for a raise, or doing more than required or expected, we need to be responsive to the situation and to other people.

Decisions in companies are often delayed far beyond what is required because those who've been asked and who are required to respond don't read the contents of their in-baskets, don't call a meeting, and don't tell the sponsors where the matter lies. Some of us make promises in an immediate attempt to please, when we know we can't deliver. Others can't deal with the issues raised when the promises they intended to keep can't be met. Still others can't say no, even when they really mean it.

A message sent deserves a response. A commitment given is to be honored or to be renegotiated. People who are responsive close open communication loops, start things, and stop things. They rarely wallow in unnecessary ambiguity, and generally they are dependable, which is key to being a successful manager and a productive person. You do what you say you will and people begin to be certain they want you in their corner. This is especially true of one's staff, but also of customers, bosses, and peers.

Why don't we naturally close? Perhaps because we tell ourselves:

"Wait, and the trouble will disappear."

"I don't want to look pushy."

"I don't want to suggest I might be the one at fault."

"I'm afraid I'll be told no."

"I don't want to hurt feelings."

To say that someone is responsive is to say that he is a person who follows through. Too many of us don't close the loop with people.

Here are some lessons that can help you become exceptionally responsive, going beyond what is generally expected. You'll find the rewards are great.

## LESSON #96

### But I Thought You Said—

Even the most apparently simple business agreement can mushroom into complexity, misunderstandings and, sometimes, rancor. Why take chances, including the chance of alienating a good relationship, when it's not necessary? Although there is no consensus on this by the experts, it's best that you confirm oral agreements in writing. Cynics might claim it's simply covering your retreat; others prefer to think of it more positively as respecting the complexity of interpersonal relationships and the difficulty of accurately communicating in the busy atmosphere of corporate life.

If a business decision, no matter how small, is serious, affecting how individuals are to work together toward a stated goal, then it's always serious enough to commit to paper. When you make such a commitment, you also are assuring others that you were listening and that you cared enough to take the time to make sure parties heard the same thing.

Sometimes, however, written confirmation may imply distrust if the receiver does not know you well, so clarify why you do it when you confirm. When agreements are in black and white in the beginning, then trust is freed up to work to get the job done.

## LESSON #97

### The Other Dreaded Pink Slip

Piles of pink telephone slips are a common sight on a manager's desk. Time flies and we can't get those calls returned. Fortunately, managers, by nature of being managers, have help.

Try to return every call the same day it's received, but if you can't, then your secretary takes over, returning a call just to let a person know when you will be able to get back to them or handling the situation so that it isn't necessary for you to call. People recognize and appreciate the extra effort. If you have an answering device on your telephone, promise the callers you'll call them back and let them know when to expect your call.

The ones who get their calls returned first, of course, should be your staff members. They not only need you, but they're on your team and are there to help you and the company be more productive. They're also the most vulnerable to being treated as second-class corporate citizens. First-class treatment will always bring out the best in them.

Of course, we all have people on our call-back list whom we would really prefer not talking to. Saying "ugh!" at the sight of particular names on message slips isn't going to make those people go away, though, and their calls should be returned just as promptly as the others. It's easy to love your friends, and it's easy to be courteous to important,

charming, intelligent, articulate, interesting people.
But, just as we should love our enemies as well, so
should we go out of our way to be polite to those to
whom we least wish to respond. If you absolutely
can't stand talking to a person, you'd better find
some other way than ignoring the call. After all,
word of such discourtesy has a way of spreading to
other relationships.

## LESSON #98

### Completing the Circle

Why is it that some managers will ask a staff
member to perform miracles on Friday in order to
provide something special on Monday? Then the
staff member works over the weekend to prepare
the requested document, turns it in on Monday, only
to see it turn yellow on the corner of the manager's
desk, with no thanks or acknowledgement of the
miracle accomplished.

At other times, a manager takes the product
created by his staff, at great personal cost in
terms of time and effort by them, and uses it
with customers or upper management. He never
bothers to tell his staff how the work was received,
whether appreciated or disliked. Thus staff members don't grow and develop from the experience,
which by the way is what any manager should be
teaching.

Then there are the many managers who receive
concrete suggestions for improvement of a process, a

report, or a technology by staff and have it instituted, but never even say thanks. Even worse is when a manager doesn't institute it *and* never acknowledges having reviewed it.

The phenomenon we are discussing is that of feedback, information returned to you that indicates whether you accomplished what you wanted to, your boss wanted you to, or your customers wanted you to. It can be a simple process. A bulletin board can contain postcards from customers both satisfied and dissatisfied. Customer surveys both internal and external to the organization are opportunities for growth and development.

Completing the circle through feedback communicates respect, motivates others for the next crisis, invites staff to respect your need for closed loops, and in the end will prevent stockpiling of negative feelings.

## LESSON #99

### Ms. Otis Regrets

I'm sure it's happened to you. You send out invitations to an event, whether social or business, and ask for a response from those invited to indicate their intent to attend. Isn't it amazing that you can't count on getting such a response from everyone invited?

In one company, the human resource department wanted to give middle managers a chance to be involved in the company's cultural change process. Each team member was responsible for sending a personal invitation to thirty middle managers to attend the orientation session they'd planned. More than 25 percent failed to respond to the RSVP. Follow-up phone calls to check on their intent were returned by fewer than 10 percent.

Except for command performances, one doesn't have to attend functions, whether at home or at work, but failing to respond to invitations, even to business functions, sends a message of disrespect to the sender.

Inconveniences to the host can also arise. A manager held a party where business associates were invited. They called and agreed to come but then didn't show up or even call to explain the circumstances. This left the manager with a surplus of refreshments and food, which didn't go well with the bad taste in his mouth.

An inviter has, as a host, a job to do and reasons for expecting a response. Ours is not to quibble with the reasons but to do our job as an invitee, the minimum of which is to respond to an RSVP—in writing when possible.

## LESSON #100

### Duly Noted

One senior manager was continually sending notes to his branch managers in praise of their production. At first blush, it seemed like a good idea. Inevitably, his managers began to compare notes, and it became obvious that the words to one person were the same as those to another. Even though his comments were handwritten, they were still impersonal, devoid of any sincerity, a shallow ritual.

Another example of such rituals is that of the manager who had been threatened with blindness and had made a miraculous recovery. A colleague of his, who had been solicitous throughout his ordeal, wrote him a note of congratulations and relief. In return, the colleague received a handwritten thank-you written in a woman's hand but with the recovered manager's signature. What the concerned colleague inferred was that he was not worth the time it would take for the manager to compose his own thank-you.

Even though a personalized note is the appropriate response in a case like this, at the very least, a typed one with the manager's signature should have been sent. Instead, what the colleague received was a note that tried to pass itself off as personal when it clearly wasn't. The result was an insult to a colleague's sincere concern and relief.

When it comes to relations between people, ritualized notes have no place. Interpersonal relationships are just that: personal. So write words that mean something to the person receiving them. And be specific. None of this "You did a good job." *What* good job? How do you really feel about it? And if you can't send a note, then telephone! Use electronic mail! Do it right, or don't bother doing it at all.

# LESSON #101

### "Boys Will Be Boys"

There is a stockbroker who leaves work at 3:00 P.M. every day to have a few drinks at a nearby bistro, and a manager who stays sloshed on the weekends but doesn't drink during the week. His spouse and children never see him, but his boss says, "He's not letting it get in the way of his work." If you believe that, I've got a bridge for you—

Some years ago at a retirement party for the group vice president, a director got so intoxicated that he became loud, boisterous, and physically out of control, falling down twice. No one said anything to him. It was a "boys will be boys" situation. Five years later, out of the blue, the same director called a consultant and desperately asked for help. The consultant went to his home to find him toxic and shaking uncontrollably. His wife was distraught and threatening to leave. The realization that his drinking was out of control, coupled with his wife's threat to leave him, had him truly frightened.

That event precipitated three hospital stays over the next five years. The company invested in his recovery, threatening the third time that he'd either have to make it or he was through. The result was that today he is an able staff member who makes a significant contribution.

He could have died while people avoided telling

him he was a sick man. He could have been confronted by his boss five years earlier instead of being enabled to continue on his path to self-destruction. His career and family life would undoubtedly have been different. A person's job is often the most important link to reality. The threat of losing a job can provide the greatest leverage for the compulsive boozer.

When you say, "Boys will be boys," or "I'm not responsible for his personal life," you are an enabler of the problem. Here are some points to keep in mind:

1. A total person works for you. Be concerned about his mental and physical health. Counsel and confront when necessary. Work is where we spend most of our time, and we need people there to care about us.
2. As the person's supervisor, you have real power—financial and career power—that can be used constructively for the staff member.
3. When you avoid dealing with the problem drinker in the name of privacy, you are really only protecting yourself from the discomfort associated with confronting the person about the problem.
4. You aren't alone in dealing with this type of problem with staff members. Get help from your boss, personnel department or others.

If you truly care about a staff member, then do whatever you can to stop their self-destruction.

## LESSON #102

### Who's *Really* on First?

One young manager had pouted through several meetings, causing his boss to finally bring him in to his office to ask what was going on. The young man burst out, "I don't think you have any regard for me, and I wonder why you want me on your team."

After some further probing, the manager found that the young man was offended that during a previous meeting requested by the young man, the manager had taken a call from a client, apologizing at the time and explaining that he'd placed a call earlier to this client and would only be a moment. During the telephone conversation, the young man had stepped out and not returned. The manager assumed that the young man had completed his business with him.

How hard it is for employees to realize that everyone is there to serve the client or customer. The personal needs of those one's company serves need to come first. To believe otherwise is to miss the purpose of it all.

In this case, the young man had not yet adopted the value that the more experienced manager held so dear, and it became a learning experience for him. But how many young men and women walk away believing that the boss doesn't have time for them because the boss let a client "get in the way"?

## LESSON #103

### How to Really Manage by Walking Around

When the idea of management by walking around became a fad, it was more a byword than a behavior. There were many barriers to its success, one being the sheer viability of senior managers of a billion-dollar, 12,000-person organization actually walking around. Who do they see? How often, in order to make it not "a strange event"?

The second barrier was that of poor training in listening. Most managers think you have to talk to your constituents, not listen. As they walked around, they would listen to the first two sentences out of a staff member's mouth, then launch into a lecture or patronizing soliloquy. The result was often catastrophic in that the staff member felt more distant than before the interchange.

The third barrier was the uncertainty of managers about what they were supposed to do if they didn't make speeches. Were they to ask about a staff member's family, fishing success, or what the person was working on, making the staff member suspicious? What were they to do when they didn't like what they heard or saw?

With these barriers, management by walking around has, if not passed out of favor, certainly faded from management's lexicon.

It's still a good idea, if it feels natural and you truly like people. But it can't be used for catching someone doing something wrong. It can't be used for giving work direction. It can't be used for making speeches. Open-ended questions followed by expressions of *true* interest—such as when, where, how, or who—will enable you to follow the other person's lead.

Such conversations, held on a regular basis, can lead to a less depersonalized leadership. However, if you find yourself breaking one of the "can't's" mentioned here, go back to your office and manage by avoiding disaffection.

## LESSON #104

### We Really Have to Stop Meeting Like This

So, there you are, buried under a stack of reports on projects and departmental budgets, a staff meeting coming up in thirty minutes, and you get a call to show up in your boss's office for "an important meeting." Pronto. When you arrive, all the department heads are there, looking equally harried and a little put out. The topic? Well, it's rather vague. Seems the big boss just wants to be filled in.

The result, as we all know, is a series of meandering, incomplete reports. No one is really prepared because no one knew in advance what to prepare for. The time is essentially wasted, and the managers are burdened with having to catch up with their other commitments.

People like to prepare for meetings or at least know the subject matter so that they can make a decision as to what they might need. When they are consistently told on the spur of the moment to come to a meeting to discuss whatever the caller wants to discuss, it becomes an inefficient use of their time—and, consequently, the company's money—and smacks of treating them like property.

Fair warning and a set agenda will encourage rather than discourage responsible participation. The same holds true for regular meetings where your staff's notes on actions taken and assignments made from the previous meeting can make the current one far more meaningful. Those attending will also think that you take the outcomes seriously. They will certainly be more responsive to their assignments under these conditions.

## LESSON #105

### I'd Like Your Input

It would appear at first glance that when someone says, "I'd like your input," it's a sincere request for a reaction to some proposition or solution to a problem. Unfortunately, it is often, or often appears to be, a sham request that people soon figure out.

Example: A hospital system administration asks the associated physicians for their input on whether to put the laboratory in Hospital A or B. After six weeks of serious discussion, the physicians recommend Hospital A and give logical reasons to support their proposition. The administration announces that Hospital B has been selected and provides little feedback to the physicians as to why. Of course, one could make a case that the administration only wanted some ideas, not a firm recommendation. If so, then they should be very specific. Asking for input can be interpreted as desiring serious recommendations.

The sham of appearing to regard others' opinions is sometimes unconscious. At other times, however, it's a manipulative strategy. Either way, the people whose opinions were requested soon get turned off and become unresponsive. The requester then becomes irritated at the apparent lack of concern when he asks for input.

When you request input, be very clear in your own mind as to how you will use it, and communicate that with the request. Input should be presented as a plan we can follow, a recommendation, alternative approaches suggested, expansions or contractions on the proposal, anything left out, any extra thoughts they might have. Then, if you choose to ignore the input, for whatever reasons, acknowledge to those who made suggestions that you appreciated the input and tell them why you chose an alternate plan.

By taking the time to acknowledge input, you lay the groundwork for an even better effort and more responsiveness the next time. Without this kind of feedback, you'll soon find the sources from which you seek input drying up, and worse, the side effects of feeling ignored will affect responsiveness to you and your actions.

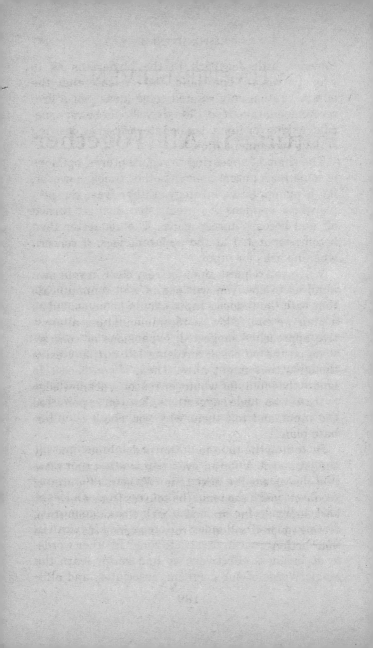

# CHAPTER ELEVEN

*

# Putting It All Together

IN THE TWENTY-FIRST century, leadership through persuasion and goodwill will replace management through power and intimidation. This ultimate expression of leadership through influence will be forced by many factors, such as the necessity to create intricate global industrial alliances, world-wide functional organizations within multinational corporations, and international banking networks. Even today such groups are more the rule than the exception.

Such complex and collaborative relationships will require a new human sensitivity and interpersonal skill that has never before been required. For example, how candid can we be? What constitutes a loss of face or dignity for associates? What does generosity mean to a New Zealander, a Korean, or a Mexican in the North American free trade zone? In other words, to do business effectively we had better learn the Magic Words of our partners, associates, and affiliates and eliminate the term "subordinates" from our vocabulary. Few people will have those hierarchies where coercive power is the primary mode of influencing behavior, decisions, and motivations. Rather, we must learn what words are "magic" for those we must influence.

However, lest this postscript suggest that the qualities we've noted are simply instrumental in nature and intended to manipulate others, we need to affirm that they are basic humanistic contentions about the dignity and worth of human beings. In other words, they are the right qualities we have come to agree on over the years.

In this emerging complicated world, ideal behaviors may vary from culture to culture even as they do between regions of the U.S. It is therefore imperative that we create explicit institutional value systems, understood by all, that lead to principles and ground rules that guide the working beliefs and behaviors of those who must collaborate with or direct others.

Obviously, the more than one hundred behaviors in this book only touch the surface of the new sensitivity the next century will demand of everyone in business and industry. It must not be forgotten that even now large and even small U.S.-based corporations often have more than 50 percent of their sales overseas. Companies such as Coca Cola and 3M have over 50 percent of their operations overseas as well. These circumstances demand that we be clear about our values, especially as they may conflict in dissatisfying ways with non–U.S.-based distributors.

As you read this book, I hope you could see how

you exercise your own values in the workplace. To what do you subscribe? How much of a discontinuity do you feel between how you treat others on the golf course or in the bowling alley and how you treat people in your office or at your work station?

Wherever you are in today's organization, you have influence over others. You either act upon the values that underlie the Magic Words or you ignore them at your peril.

I recently asked my dentist why he always said "please" and "thank you" when he directed his dental assistant to hand him one of those wicked tools or terrible tasting solutions. After some reflection, he said, "I believe in showing respect to my associates, and I know if we show consideration to each other we'll do the same to our patients." In the competitive twenty-first century, trust, fairness, generosity, respect, consideration, gratefulness, dignity, integrity, candor, and responsiveness won't only be right; they'll be good business.

# INDEX

\*

293